D1483079

THE ARTIST IN HIS STUDIO

Also by Alexander Liberman
GREECE, GODS, AND ART

THE ARTIST IN HIS STUDIO

TEXT AND PHOTOGRAPHS
BY ALEXANDER LIBERMAN

WITH A FOREWORD BY JAMES THRALL SOBY

A STUDIO BOOK
THE VIKING PRESS: NEW YORK

PUBLISHED IN 1960 BY THE VIKING PRESS, INC.
625 MADISON AVENUE, NEW YORK, N.Y. 10022
PUBLISHED SIMULTANEOUSLY IN CANADA BY
THE MACMILLAN COMPANY OF CANADA LIMITED
REISSUED 1968 IN REDUCED FORMAT
IN HARDCOVER AND SOFTCOVER EDITIONS

PORTIONS OF THIS BOOK APPEARED IN *Vogue*

LIBRARY OF CONGRESS CATALOG CARD NUMBER: 60-13244
PRINTED IN U.S.A.

CONTENTS

ACKNOWLEDGMENTS

This book, in preparation for ten years, was made possible by the sustained enthusiasm of my colleagues, the editors of *Vogue*. In its pages ten of these essays, now considerably enlarged and revised, first appeared, with some of the accompanying photographs.

I wish to acknowledge with gratitude the help of: Iva S. V.-Patcévitch, the publisher of *Vogue* and president of the Condé Nast Publications, for his deep interest and understanding; Jessica Daves, editor-in-chief of *Vogue,* for her continued encouragement; Allene Talmey, senior editor of *Vogue,* for her faith, judgment, and invaluable contribution to the editing of the texts and material; Priscilla Peck, art editor of *Vogue,* for her perceptive advice and enthusiasm in the project from its inception.

In addition, I wish to thank The Museum of Modern Art and, among its trustees and staff: James Thrall Soby, Alfred H. Barr, Jr., Monroe Wheeler, and Edward Steichen. It was the Museum's exhibition of many of these photographs, *The Artist in His Studio,* that led directly to this book. Special acknowledgment is due William S. Lieberman for his conception of that exhibition and for his advice in the planning of the book; and to Charlotte Trowbridge Dyer for her beautiful design of the Museum's exhibition and her knowing help on the book.

My thanks go as well to Francine du Plessix Gray, my daughter, for her devoted aid in the first years of the project, and to Phyllis Starr, Marcel Guillaume, Charles O. Hyman, Edmund Winfield, and Gladys Pohl for their valuable assistance in their fields.

And, a final indispensable expression of gratitude to my mother, who first instilled, and then furthered throughout my life, a passion for art and painting.

FOREWORD

Alexander Liberman is unique among contemporary photographers in the stead-
fastness of his documentary purpose—to record and interpret with a camera the
personalities and *ambiance* of some of the leading European painters and sculptors of our time. Other photographers have undertaken the same fascinating task,
of course, but usually as an excursion into portraiture or as one among many
subjects that have interested them. Liberman, on the contrary, has gone to France
for several months each year since 1947, and there has made endless photographs
of members of the School of Paris, their homes, their studios. He has brought to
this work not only an extraordinary visual sensitivity (he is himself an estimable
painter and sculptor), but also a rare capacity for psychological insight, as anyone
must be aware who has read his essays.

An essential quality of any true artist is separateness, whether he works in
defiant solitude or within the discipline of an established style. Liberman has
caught this quality time after time, so that in variety, range, and penetration his
photographs create a pageantry in which the figures and accessories are altogether
memorable, each in its own way. The result has been an invaluable enrichment
of our knowledge of modern painters and sculptors, what they are like and about.
And even if art history could be put aside for a moment, these photographs would
still be sheer pleasure to look at and look at repeatedly, without that gradual or
quick abatement of interest so often felt in viewing photographic exhibitions and
albums.

JAMES THRALL SOBY

TO TATIANA, MY WIFE

INTRODUCTION

During the last war, when France became a battlefield, I feared that many traces of a heroic epoch might vanish. Since the Renaissance in Italy, no country except France has seen such a continued flourishing of painting and sculpture. After the war, I decided to seek out those artists who had contributed most to this modern renaissance. My book includes only artists who have lived in France during the last hundred years, only painters and sculptors who have been closely connected with the School of Paris. Many were alive, many still are. These I visited. The remaining traces of those who were dead I sought out.

The more I explored, the more absorbed I became with the mystery of environment. Why should France have become the focal center of painting and sculpture at this particular time? What relationship exists between the painting and the vision of reality that daily the artist has before his eyes? At no time have I believed that environment is a complete explanation of art. I am sure, however, that it plays an important role. Further I cannot go, but I can offer to artists, historians, and other readers this record of how some of the greatest painters and sculptors of our time have looked, lived, and worked. I tried to reveal the core of their creative act, to show the creative process itself, and thereby to relate painting and sculpture with the mainstream of man's search for truth. Painters and sculptors, like poets or scientists, are seekers of truth.

In books on art I found little factual information about artists' studios, methods of work, and tools. The books concentrate on either biography or aesthetics. Seldom has anyone described those details that are part of the creation of the work of art itself. One reason is that the studios of great painters are seldom preserved intact after their deaths. Even if some are preserved, or made into museums, the "cleaning-up" usually destroys the link with the artists. However, with most studios I was fortunate; Cézanne's, for instance, was still more or less as he had left it. I looked at the studios with the painter's interest in mind. Whenever I saw a significant detail that added to my fuller knowledge of the artist and his method of work I recorded it. To document the creative act I had to observe it without altering it by my presence. To gain the confidence of an artist, so that he could work as if I were not in the studio, took several years of patient visits.

Sometimes the artist himself is ignored while the spotlight focuses upon his work. Sometimes he dies or becomes very old before his work is recognized. I tried to catch expressions that seemed to have meaning in connection with temperament and creativity—especially those of artists such as Rouault, Kupka, and Villon, who had to wait until they were over seventy for recognition. About these men there has been relatively little recorded, in contrast with Picasso, more amply documented than any painter in history.

This book is not intended as a thorough, systematic study of modern art history or a compilation of biographical data. It is a series of impressions, essays in words and photographs. Some important artists are not represented because of the physical impossibility of including everyone, but I hope that through the ones who do appear the essential atmosphere of the epoch will show. The unequal space given to each artist is not meant in any way to diminish or increase his relative importance. In many instances this variance depended on the amount of available material, the amount of time I was given by the artist, and sometimes on my personal affinity with the man and his work. It is on this subjective plane that my book might be best approached. I hope that it will communicate some of my admiration for the men and women who have created the revolution of modern art.

After years spent in visiting, talking to, and photographing these great artists, I am impressed most by their obsessive, unswerving dedication to creation. In the words of the poet, they are "a lifetime burning." Their dedication to art, like that of men to religious orders, is a self-imposed vow. These artists are the priests of a new religion—Art. Jacques Villon, the grand old master of modern art, at the age of eighty-four said to me in 1959, "Before starting to paint one should follow Cennini's advice and say a prayer." The long history of painting has come full cycle, for Cennino Cennini, in the fourteenth century, defined the chief virtues that a man taking up painting should have: "Therefore, you who love this accomplishment because of a refined disposition, which is the chief reason for your engaging in our art, begin by adorning yourselves with these vestments: love, reverence, obedience, and perseverance."

A. L., NEW YORK, 1960

NOTE TO THE NEW EDITION

In the eight years since the first edition of this book several of the artists have died: Arp (1966), Giacometti (1966), Le Corbusier (1965), Gontcharova (1962), Larionov (1964), Braque (1963), Pevsner (1962), Villon (1963), Van Dongen (1968).

I have not changed any of the text. To do so, I felt, would alter the mood in which the essays devoted to these artists were originally written, and thus change the spirit of the book.

A. L., NEW YORK, 1968

10

I

IMPRESSIONISTS AND POST-IMPRESSIONISTS

CÉZANNE RENOIR MONET BONNARD

CÉZANNE

Paul Cézanne is the spiritual father of modern art. His pictorial lessons and discoveries are more than ever alive in the art of our time. He is the painters' painter. His personal struggle to reconcile the two realities of an artist's existence, the life of art and the life of man, provides an ideal study of the artist as a phenomenon of existence. Cézanne is an archetype for painters.

He was a rich man. He once said, "My father was a man of genius. He left me an income of twenty-five thousand francs." Thus Cézanne never had to worry about material existence. He could afford to live without having to sell his art. This independence was one of the great secrets of Cézanne's liberty, and he knew it well. Throughout his life his gratitude and admiration for his father never ceased.

For a long time the modern movements in art have been associated in the mind of the uninformed public with Bohemianism, revolution, disorder. Cézanne disproves this legend. A rich bourgeois, he lived a humble, methodical, solitary life. The house he built himself in Aix-en-Provence around 1902 is a somber shell that still stands today on the rechristened Avenue Paul Cézanne. I found little difference between the modest two-story building and its neighboring suburban houses when I visited it in 1949; only the immense studio that occupies the whole second story distinguishes it. The house is still intact more than fifty years after Cézanne's death. By an accident of fate it was bought by a Provençal poet who lived in the lower rooms and did not touch the studio itself. Today Cézanne's beret, his cape, his paint boxes, his rosary, his palettes and bottles of turpentine, all the objects that surrounded him during his work are there as he left them, untouched, unmoved throughout the years.

Two tiny rooms, a dark dining room and a bedroom, open out onto the tile floor of the little entrance hall. Alongside the dining room is a dark kitchen in which one can barely move. The proportion of the three rooms is the minimum essential for a retired functionary. A minuscule staircase with a metal balustrade and a wooden ramp winds up in a slow curve to the second floor. In contrast to the dinginess and the smallness of the living quarters the studio is luminous, tall, high, and, as in many painters' houses, obviously the center, the principal room in the man's life. The studio is extremely orderly, with its meticulously kept filing cabinets, books, papers, and a long shelf on which Cézanne had arranged with method the objects that inspired him. The great height of this

11

austere room is accentuated by a small crucifix which is hung close to the ceiling.

This is the studio of his old age, a dynamic old age in which Cézanne created some of his greatest masterpieces. His *Les Grandes Baigneuses,* now in Philadelphia, was finished in this room after seven years' work. The longevity of painters is striking. Cézanne died at sixty-seven, Matisse at eighty-five, Rouault at eighty-seven, Léger at seventy-four, Kupka at eighty-six, Kandinsky at seventy-eight; Villon is eighty-five, Picasso is seventy-nine. Such longevity contradicts the established legend that the artist destroys himself. The stimulus of creation seems to be favorable to the human system; perhaps boredom and lack of activity kill faster than the difficulties of creative living. In their old age all these painters have kept the spark of youth. Cézanne's friend Gasquet wrote that when he visited Mont Sainte-Victoire with Cézanne at sixty-five, he said, "This is like the first spring."

This studio, stark and sad, a room of anguish and torment, was also the shell of a hardened egotist. Cézanne sacrificed all personal human contacts to achieve his vision. Bitterly, indestructibly egotistical, he forced his wife to live apart from him and treated his friends indifferently. There is not a single comfortable or luxurious object in his house. All is centered around work. Like Picasso, the richest contemporary painter, Cézanne lived in ascetic, mystical surroundings, with painting as his sole luxury. Yet, like Braque, Cézanne had the means to materialize his conception of the ideal workroom. There is similarity between Braque, Picasso, and Cézanne in the uncluttered space of their working areas. There is space and grandeur in their studios; in the act of planning them, they preconceived the immensity of their purpose. Cézanne's conception was vast; one can still see the slit knocked out on the wall of his studio through which his *Baigneuses,* too large to go through the doors or windows, was taken out.

By the far wall away from the crucifix is a stove with a long pipe to heat the immense studio. Gasquet recalls that one of Cézanne's greatest paintings, the *Old Woman with a Rosary,* which he did one year before his death, was found lying next to the stove, steam dripping down on it. Cézanne, seeking the summit of art, was often in despair with his own achievement. He slashed, threw, stamped on canvases, folded them to prop up a sideboard, tossed them out of windows. Vollard remembers once seeing a canvas hanging on a tree near his studio. This disregard for his creation, a mixture of pride and intense humility, was one of the conflicts of Cézanne's life. He knew his greatness.

Hanging on hooks in the farthest corner of his studio are a thick black woolen coat with a cape, his beret, another coat, a folding easel, a white parasol and a canvas bag smeared with oil paint, all living souvenirs of his contacts with the outdoors. He had great physical energy and walked miles through the countryside to his motif. He identified himself and his canvas with his landscape, in the most literal sense of communicating with nature. His studio was a study into which he brought the riches that he collected outside, to write them down in color and line into the scientific journal which was his painting. "Everything is in art, especially theory developed and applied in contact with nature."

This artist was born in Aix and died in Aix; except for infrequent trips to Paris and visits with his friends, he seldom left his birthplace. It was the profound

miliarity between his eye and his surroundings that permitted Cézanne to see
ie nature around him as though he were seeing into himself. One of the secrets
iat we attribute to genius may be merely acute observation. How often one says,
)oking at a painting, "What a genius this man is to have interpreted the shadow
s blue!" But the fact is that, in a particular geographic location, the shadow
ctually is blue. If Cézanne had not been so deeply rooted in his Aix country-
ide and had not for over half a century observed its shadows, he might not have
endered them as precisely as he did. In old age Cézanne would allow himself
he luxury of being driven in a fiacre to the subject he wanted to paint. He
vould stop the driver and say, "Look at these blues—look at these blues under
he pine tree." And in the countryside of Aix, the blues that Cézanne was the
irst to see are there today for anyone to see.

Cézanne's unwillingness to travel, to change, is in striking contrast to the
idventurous spirit of many artists. "My eyes are stuck to the point I look upon,"
ie said. "I feel they would bleed if I tore them away." This fixity of vision and
ecognition of the infinite richness within small changes are revelations of
Cézanne's method. There may be a link between Cézanne's power of concen-
ration and (without intention of a pun) his concentric conception of vision.
'It became concentric by looking and working," he said. He wanted to show
nature composed of "the cylinder, the sphere, the cone." These forms are based
on the circle, and this revolutionary discovery is one of his profound contribu-
tions. To Leonardo da Vinci's statement, "The eye is the top of a pyramid,"
Cézanne might have answered, "The eye is the top of a cone." To Cézanne, a
base was not linear but curvilinear. In his obsession with apples, with fruit, with
his baroque-tormented arabesques of the human form, the future father of cubism
tried to break the static linear volume into a flowing curvilinear rhythm.

His obsession with Mont Sainte-Victoire, the rock mountain that stands
like a cathedral dominating the plain of Aix, involved much more than a pictorial problem. In contemplating this manifestation of nature, unspoiled by man,
Cézanne sought more than a communion with the Creator, he wanted to be the
hand and the eye of the Creator: "I want to paint," he said, "the virginity of
the world." In seeking the secret rhythm underlying creation, Cézanne was seeking the universal, the eternal, the classic, for his was no expressionistic ego playing with accident. Cézanne is the great classicist. His heads tend toward one
common basic shape, which is the underlying unity that he was striving to reveal.
The exact shape of a particular head is but an accident; he sought the basic,
universal form of the human head. The mountain, to his eye, was like minute
life revealed through a microscope, the gigantic, visible revelations of nature's
rhythms and structures. After this vision, Cézanne could see in a humble tablecloth a smaller symbol of the same life-pattern; the folds of a napkin in one of
his still lifes have the grandeur of Mont Sainte-Victoire. The eye of the spectator
travels and recognizes within the lines of any great still life, portrait, or landscape
the eternal movement that it subconsciously seeks, and is satisfied. The painting
possessed with the rhythms of nature itself becomes a part of creation, an object
of nature.

Cézanne's great good fortune may have been that he remained on the outskirts of Aix, so deeply immersed in nature. Painters who live in cities seem

gradually to accept the transitory as reality. City streets, cars, factories, theaters, momentarily hide the real aspects of nature from city-dwellers. Anything man-made is not eternal. As Cézanne well understood, it is only in nature undefiled by man that eternal truth can be discovered. The artists of the cities are also frequently spoiled by money and success. It may be that the continuity of Cézanne's vision lay in his isolation, his lack of appreciation by the public of his time. He pursued art, regardless of recognized success. He may have occasionally craved the satisfaction of approval, but his proud nature revolted against his bourgeois-dominated age.

Cézanne carried his love of nature to the people who lived in nature. His friends were the gardeners, the farmers, the peasants; he helped them live, gave them money, painted their portraits. He fought bitterly against the narrow-minded middle class and, being close to the humble people of his native Aix, remained close to their basic tastes and understanding.

The peasants who were Cézanne's friends and models were also his link with the truth of nature. Just as the Mont Sainte-Victoire remained undefiled by human hands, these simple people were unspoiled by false culture. From their rough, weathered faces, Cézanne could paint his human landscapes.

Hanging on the studio walls are cheap, bad reproductions of his favorite artists, El Greco, Tintoretto, Titian, Delacroix, Courbet. Cézanne wanted to redo the classics, "redo Poussin after nature." He did not discard the lessons of the past masters, but retaught these lessons to advance human vision a step further. A classicist, Cézanne did not break with tradition; he developed tradition within the spirit of his time. All artists whose influence has been lasting have based their work on an idea, a philosophical concept. Renaissance art was above all an intellectual revolution based on the discovery of humanism; the impressionists found their sources in the optical revolution of Chevreul. In Cézanne's life, as in his work, he sought method. He once said of Rodin, "What he lacks is a cult, a system, a faith."

On a long, high shelf stand the objects he used so many times in his still lifes: Puget's *Amour,* the *écorché,* the straw-bound bottle, the vases, the bowls. In their carefully preserved accumulation these everyday objects are the standards of comparison with his works. The measure of his departure from these objects reveals his theories. Cézanne's acceptance of the reality of nature, of man, of the objects that surrounded him was part of the naturalistic revolution of the early twentieth century. Nature, naturalism are essentials in Cézanne's work. He is one of the greatest modern painters because he taught artists to portray their own time, to avoid an outdated mythology, and to create their own myth.

The ceiling of the studio is white, the doors pale gray, the walls slate-gray. The floor of natural unvarnished wood, gray with age, adds a warmer shade to the monochromatic room. Almost all the colors that surrounded Cézanne were gray—part of his need of subtle, unviolent color within which he could see all modulations. "Gray alone reigns in nature," he said, "but it's frightfully difficult to catch." No one saw more colors in a gray than Cézanne. And the dark gray walls of his studio are the neutral background against which his eye translated the many hues of his inner vision. This great colorist also loved to paint on a gray day.

"Light is a thing that cannot be reproduced," he said, "but must be represented by something else—by color. I was pleased with myself when I discovered that." This interchangeability of light and color is similar to the modern notion of charges of energy. When Cézanne said, "The painter is above all an optic," he meant that the artist vibrates under the energy impulse of color and translates the charge onto the canvas.

Two tall bottles stand on a shelf still half-filled with turpentine, darkened with age, reminders of Cézanne's mediums. He thinned his paints more than any other painter, trying to reduce density of color for a less material but more important use. Cézanne's method prefigured the research of contemporary painting. Before him color was looked upon as the property of the object painted, as part of its substance. The orange of an orange belonged to the orange itself. But Cézanne with his translucent, transparent tones tried to put into his water colors and his oils a light from behind; his white canvas or white paper charges his thin film of color with an inner glow. The uncovered areas of his canvases are his affirmation that the canvas is the light behind color.

On a piece of glass Cézanne mixed his colors, often adding gray—no pure colors but a swirling, subtle mixture of subdued tints. From this impromptu palette one can judge the energy, the impulsiveness of the painter at the moment of creation. On this palette he was free to let his hand move with undisciplined passion. In this freedom he found a release before again disciplining his passion into the methodic, systematic strokes that are the substance of his painting. Passion, mysticism, discipline, anguish are still felt in this room whose occupant died fifty-four years ago. It remains charged with the intense radiation that his energy infused into all he touched. For Braque, who said, "I like the rule that corrects emotion," Cézanne is the Gospel. His whole life was the rule that corrected emotion. From all accounts, there was a constant struggle in Cézanne between his passionate, romantic nature and his conception of art. Somewhere inside he was an expressionist with a constant desire to pour out his feelings in violent images. Only his admiration for classical art and his high conception of the artist's mission could discipline him. This struggle led Cézanne to the high summits of classical art, in which his ego was vanquished, but not without the struggle needed for great creation. The artist suffers, strives, but the work of art is pure, serene, calm, and eternal. Cézanne's apples and portraits have the eternal repose that fulfills our need of permanence. The solidity of Mont Sainte-Victoire, encased in an atmosphere formed of the same molecules as the mountain, conveys that satisfaction of permanence.

Cézanne had the infinite patience to build a system which would translate what he saw. Painting had suffered under improvisation, under so-called inspiration, and compared with music and writing it had relatively no laws. Cézanne created the most demanding and rigorous pictorial system devised by man.

Attached to a small wooden rosary are a crucifix and a small skull. These are links with one of Cézanne's favorite painters, El Greco, in whose portraits of prelates and saints there is often a skull, symbolizing the presence of death. Cézanne's Catholic mysticism drove him into the solitary meditation of a monk. His was the freedom of the iconoclast to break with tradition, but to break with tradition he had to be very familiar with that with which he broke. The cheap reproductions of past masters in his studio were his links with the past. Cézanne also had the means, in the early materialistic twentieth century, to meditate in a self-mad monastery. He could afford the luxury of living like a hermit, afford to resis violently all interruptions, all attempts of dealers to put the hand on him.

It is only in a life of peace and silence that one can see clearly, that one ca even attempt what Cézanne attempted: a vision of the over-all pattern of creation Cézanne's vision was close to that of another mystic, Spinoza, who wrote, "Go and the universal laws of structure and operation are one and the same reality." Cézanne's answer to a friend who asked him if he believed was "If I did not believ I could not paint." And he once said of a sculptor, "He makes admirable piece: but he does not see the whole." This vision of the whole belongs only to genius. I is said that Mozart could visualize his music as though it were a painting, coul see the whole in one moment of time while other composers conceived their wor within the passage of time. The whole is another form of harmony, which is th planned relationship of various parts, and to see the plan one must have a perspec tive, a distance of vision so that he is not lost in detail. Cézanne, who said, "Natur to me is very complex," needed the perspective given by meditation and faith t unravel the complexity of sensation.

Several skulls lying on shelves are evidence of Cézanne's need for permanency As God's creation has permanency, as the human skull remains behind as a re minder of life, so painting needs that solid structure that will preserve it throug time. This demand for structure, this bone of Cézanne's vision, is similar to Plato' system of ideas. Cézanne admired Plato, who over his academy placed the inscrip tion, "Let no man ignorant of geometry enter here." Cézanne wrote, "God alway geometrizes."

The security based on number is one of the reasons for music's emergence a a major art. And Cézanne's greatness lies in this seeking for universal law an permanent rhythm through number. In his search for solidity, for the perceptio of universal harmony, he was conscious of musical ends. "To paint," he said, "i not to copy slavishly the object . . . it is to seize harmony between several corres pondences, then to transpose them into a scale of one's own and to develop them following a new and original logic." So he used the harmonic principles of music trying to establish for the art of painting the structural security and solidity tha is particular to music. When Cézanne said, "I will have to repaint this whol portrait if I put in one accidental stroke," he was a musician afraid of a false note

The concept of "idea" has changed in our modern world. When artist speak of ideas today they do not use the word in a Platonic or Cézannian sens but in a literary sense. No one hated literary painting more than Cézanne. Fo Cézanne storytelling was not the way to great and universal painting. For him t tend toward an idea was to tend toward the ideal, the essence of a thing. "Natur for us is revealed more in depth than in surface," he said. His ideal was so great his purpose so immense, that if he sometimes deprecated his own achievement i was not, as many thought, because he was afraid he lacked talent; it was his feelin of unworthiness before his Creator.

The garden outside his house, with its geranium pots and olive trees, stil stands beside the quiet lane leading down to the city of Aix, which so long ignore him. Mont Sainte-Victoire still stands. The eternal nature, from which the acci dental spark that was Cézanne has disappeared, remains eternal. But his painting remain engraved in memory like a revelation of the truth about ourselves that we knew but did not face. And one of those noble silver olive trees must have been his friend, of whom he said to Gasquet, "It's a living human, it knows all of my life and gives me wonderful advice. I would like to be buried at its feet." It is said that Cézanne often came out to speak to the tree and embrace it.

NOTES ON THE ILLUSTRATIONS

Paul Cézanne. 1839–1906. Born, France.
Photographs taken in 1949.

1 A view of Mont Sainte-Victoire, one of Cézanne's most constant themes, from the outskirts of Aix-en-Provence. The magnificent architecture of the rocks obsessed the painter preoccupied with the mystery of nature's relation to art.

2 This is the room where modern art was born, one of the holy places of painting: the last studio Cézanne built for himself, in 1902, on the Chemin des Lauves near Aix. Here, before his death, he felt the first glow of world recognition. Here he painted his masterpiece, *Les Grandes Baigneuses,* in seven years. Finished, it was so large that an opening had to be made in a wall to get it out. On the left hang his coats, capes, berets, and his painting satchel. On the long shelf above are many objects Cézanne used in his still lifes. In the foreground is the table on which he made his arrangements. The wooden mannequin is a reminder of how hard it was for him to get models to pose in the nude. The walls were still the original rich, subtle gray that Cézanne interpreted with infinite subtlety in the grays of his paintings, grays achieved through many colors.

3 *Portrait of the Artist,* c. 1885. Pencil on white paper, $13'' \times 10\frac{3}{4}''$. Collection Walter Cummings Baker, New York.

4 On a shelf next to his charcoal sticks, three skulls. Cézanne used a skull in several of his paintings as a reminder of the structure and death underlying life.

5 The raw materials of great art: a jar, a wine bottle, a glass, and Puget's *Amour,* all now imprinted in our memory as transformed by Cézanne's art.

6 *The Bathers,* 1902–1903. Oil, $28\frac{3}{4}'' \times 36\frac{1}{4}''$. Private collection.

RENOIR

Les Collettes, Auguste Renoir's villa in Cagnes on the French Riviera, is the tangible trace left of the master's way of life. His studio, once a glass construction in the garden, was so badly damaged by a bomb in the last war that it had to be destroyed. The villa is a large one with terraces, regal in comparison with the simple dwellings of most artists. The nineteenth-century bourgeois elegance and formality of its interior remind one of the artistic conventions with which Renoir had to break.

Along the main drive up to the entrance of the villa, palm trees add their stylization of form to that of several Renoir sculptures. The magnificent century-old olive trees that Renoir painted so many times are like human bodies writhing in space, bathed by the scintillating reflections of sunlight through their silvery leaves. When the mist rises from the sea and softens the blinding Mediterranean light, the subtlest hues of color become intensified. If one stops to meditate in this landscape, the vision of Renoir emerges. His search, a classical one of the artist, was to incorporate man into nature, for nature, however beautiful, does not give a sense of total fulfillment without a fusion by the artist of the human and inhuman.

Renoir moved to Cagnes in 1903 and died there in 1919 at the age of seventy-eight. Toward the end of his life he suffered severely from rheumatism and had to be wheeled about in a chair. His arms, however, were not crippled, and he painted with brushes tied to his pain-knotted hands. It was during this time at Cagnes that he developed the grand style of his late period. Freed from the doubts of youth, freed from the need of scholarly discipline, he invented a new intensity of form and color. He had reached the knowledge that "Regularity, order, desire for perfection (which is always false perfection) destroy art. . . . Irregularity is the basis of all art." This freeing of a painter's vision is the moment of revelation that some great painters reach in their long lives. Renoir was one of the fortunate geniuses who live long enough to begin to see what they search all their lives to see.

NOTES ON THE ILLUSTRATIONS

Auguste Renoir, 1841–1919. Born, France.
Photographs taken in 1957.

7 The olive trees and the luxurious vegetation that surround Renoir's house in Cagnes-sur-Mer on the French Riviera. This is the vision of nature from which he drew his last inspirations. Renoir is, above all, the painter of the human form, but like the great masters of the past he attempted the fusion of body and flesh with the elemental forces of nature, fire, air, water, earth, made possible by the miracle of light.

8 The living room of Les Collettes. Toward the end of his life, Renoir, because of acute rheumatism, had to spend more and more time in the south. Here, in this house, he lived a calm, organized, bourgeois existence surrounded by his large family. In the dining room next to the living room, many simple wood chairs around the vast table are reminders of the children and grand-children who animated the quiet of his last retreat.

9 *Mlle Henriot,* Oil, 21⅝″ × 18⅛″. Collection O. Reinhart, Winterthur.

MONET

In 1883 Claude Monet settled in Giverny, a small village on the river Epte, seventy kilometers from Paris; and here, until his death in 1926 at the age of eighty-six, the true founder of impressionism lived and worked in comfort and seclusion.

The image of Monet that the world remembers is the one of him, in the Giverny gardens, in the blue coat and trousers of a gardener, a large hat shielding his eyes from the sun. His piercing eyes peer from this shade like those of a hunter, protected by the leafy shadow, observing his prey. Below the dark, deep shadow across his face, the white patriarchal beard gleams whiter.

Monet's house and studio have been lovingly preserved by his son, Michel, who lives nearby. Actually living on the place is Monet's stepson, a small, alert old man with a long white beard, who, dressed in the blue overalls of a head gardener, walked with me through the blue-shaded gravel paths. Twenty-eight years after Claude Monet's death, the descendants of the flowers that watched him were surrounding this man, who looked like a materialization of Monet. The white beard created the illusion of time standing still; it was the mysterious, unexpected visual accent that suddenly, like the tuning of an orchestra, gives the right note, synchronizes our sensations, focuses them in the proper channel in order that we may fully experience. The white of the beard, when struck by the sun against the background orgy of violent colors, was a rest, a pause like an uncovered area of a painting through which the pure white of the canvas shows.

A long, low two-storied structure, Monet's house reminded me of the gaily painted railway stations of small French summer resorts. The vivid emerald-green paint of the windows intensified the complementary red paint of the brickwork; large bands of white underscored the banal architecture, the gay colors integrating the building into the tapestry of the garden.

That vast garden of Giverny became his outdoor studio. The Monet garden is a symbol of an era—a moment in history when peace seemed eternal, prosperity guaranteed by science and progress. The early struggles of impressionism were over; Monet, the successful artist, could literally live in his own impressionistic landscape. Here, "nature imitated art." The carefully planted trees, the long *allées,* created depths and perspectives.

But the true meaning of this garden was in the flowers. On that summer day the intense colors of the flowers forced me to stop as though pushed back by their tangible color radiations. The air seemed full of color waves; I blinked, the brief darkness a necessary relief. A step forward seemed possible only under the cover of that momentary darkness. The buzzing of insects underscored the waves of visual sound. In this laboratory of sensual pleasures the colors and sounds entrapped us.

The flowers were planted with apparent carelessness, irregular masses of yellow floating next to patches of climbing pinks and reds in a sea of green. Proust, who used Monet as the model for the painter Elstir in his *Remembrance of Things Past,* had written of Monet's garden: "a garden of hues and colors more than flowers; a garden that is less the old flower garden but a color garden."

Of color Monet said, "When you go out to paint, try to forget what objects you have before you, a tree, a house, a field, or whatever. Merely think, here is a little square of blue, here an oblong of pink, here a streak of yellow, and paint it just as it looks to you, the exact color and shape, until it gives you your own naïve impression of the scene before you."

This vast estate was like a giant nursery in which plants, trees, flowers were but the fertilizer for that mysterious growth, painting. Scattered, independent studio buildings were hothouses in which the slow creative germination of inspiration could take place. The original visual inspiration born outdoors was brought back to the glass studio, where, like a seedling, it would grow hidden from the real world until, full grown, it was a painting.

After we left the brilliance of the outdoors, the enormous studio was dark and austere. The immense panoramic water-lily canvases, leaning against the walls, glowed against the grayness. Covering the well of the narrow staircase leading to his room were hundreds of Japanese woodcuts, their blue dominants vibrating against the acid pink of tall fireweed at the entrance door.

We walked from the studio over to the house. Inside and intact were traces of a comfortable bourgeois life. The all-yellow dining room, its walls densely hung with more Japanese prints, was a place of enjoyment. Monet's stepson said, "Nothing was ever spicy enough for him." The blue-aquamarine-green accents of the evenly spaced prints spotted the chrome-yellow walls like an iridescent collection of rare butterflies.

In the salon were photographs, bibelots, and the quiet dignity of rooms formally arranged, but not truly inhabited. For in this house life was obviously elsewhere. Monet paintings hung in several rows on the walls, their watery greenness made more intense by the green reflections of the emerald shutters. On tables were blocks of crystal and pale Japanese prints and, like offerings in an ancestor cult, freshly cut flowers, placed by his sons in the many vases scattered around the dark room.

The center of the house, with a few steps leading to the small iron-grilled door, was the axis for the principal allée of the garden. A series of iron arches encased that allée in a flowered grip. Those arches, now partly uncovered, poked their rusty skeletons through the masses of climbing roses; metal, rust, flowers, a curious funereal association, with yet a suggestion of a country fair in the naïve humor of these triumphant arches.

To enter Monet's most private garden with its extraordinary Oriental water-lily pond, we had to cross the railroad tracks that cut through his meditative, tender, and flowered landscape. Those tracks sliced through the two garden worlds of Claude Monet—the French impressionist garden and the Buddhist water-lily pond.

Around the pond the all-pervading green gave a monochromatic sensation. This one-color dominant allowed him a visual rest and a concentration on deeper values. His pond was the culmination of Monet's lifetime interest in Japanese art.

Oriental art, which gave a direct impetus to Monet and impressionism, can be fully understood only through the knowledge of Zen. Truth cannot be understood, it must be felt. Each one must seek it for himself and find it himself; nothing can be taught. One of the fundamentals of Zen is that it is impossible to describe in words that which it is most important to say.

Tao is the way of nature, the universal order; the Oriental artist seeks it in contact with nature, and that is why landscapes are a favorite theme. Occidentals make a great mistake if, in the art of China and Japan, they see an impressionistic study of mountains and lakes. The Oriental artist, in a state of meditation, expresses a deeper truth through such familiar visible symbols.

Since symbols are abstractions, the seemingly realistic art of the Orient is actually an abstract painting in which the symbols used have the appearance of reality. The waterfall stands for a "symbol of continuous movement, a symbol of the world in which elements constantly change, but form remains unchanged."

To practice Tao is to live according to nature, to accept it as the all-pervading force of the universe. Man must comply with it and not seek to dominate it. Humility of man, humility of nature are essential for a harmonious existence. Water, which always seeks the low places, is a visual symbol of this belief. Water always held a fascination for Monet. In its transparent liquid density he saw a tangible materialization of that invisible air that bathed the nature he painted. Water became a liquid air. The ever-changing states of water, like a flexible optical system, helped Monet and his colleagues to see the structure of light.

It was to be Monet's destiny to investigate deeply some of the major preoccupations of contemporary art: the Orient, light, color, and abstraction. The great re-evaluation of Claude Monet, taking place today, is due to his prescience. Toward the end of his life, blinded by cataracts, Monet, the great visionary of light, was again as desperate as in the heroic days of impressionism.

People sometimes forget how impressionism came about. Claude Monet, who became the undisputed leader of the new movement, was born in Paris, the son of a grocer. His childhood was spent in Le Havre, the great French Channel port. At sixteen he drew caricatures with such success that one of them was noticed at a frame-dealer's by the painter Eugène Boudin. He initiated the young Monet, making him a disciple of his faith that art needs nature and that the studio must be abandoned for the direct contact with the living light of the outdoors.

Monet became part of a group of artists who regularly came to the Channel beaches to paint—Boudin, Jongkind. The seascapes that they painted were studies of space, color, and light—a realistic attempt to render the until then unpainted atmosphere. This air, this ether that bathes all nature, was here rendered more visible by the presence of water.

The two years of military service that Monet spent at the age of twenty in North Africa were to play a decisive role in his perceptions; like Eugène Delacroix, the great colorist, he had found in the light and color of Africa the answer to his thirst for new visual sensations. Monet said, "The impressions of light and color that I received there were not to classify themselves until later; they contained the germ of my future researches."

When, after an illness, he returned to France, there he met, and through the years became inseparable from, all the men who were to become his companions in the struggle for a new art—Manet, Renoir, Degas, Pissarro, Sisley, Cézanne. These men, under the influences of Delacroix's color and Courbet's realism and Corot's vision of nature, led the revolt against academic art with its dirty-brown imitation of old masters.

At the 1867 Paris World's Fair they came in contact with Japanese art. This vision of the world with its conception and techniques of art, new to the artists of France, had a deep lasting effect on all the Occidental artists. The Japanese engravings were to have the same revolutionary effect on the creative thinking of the impressionists as Negro sculpture had later on the cubists.

In 1874 Monet exhibited a painting, *Impression, Sunrise*. The academic critics seized on his word and from then on "impressionism" as a derogatory label clung to Monet and his friends. To be an impressionist one had to have strength of character, for this new art was ridiculed and insulted. At one time Monet, desperately poor, thought of suicide, but his courage returned. Eventually he had the acclaim of those who had earlier condemned his work. Finally rich, he bought his house in Giverny.

He lived long enough there to feel again out of fashion. The last years of his life were saddened by the lack of understanding that surrounded his final creative research, the great series of *Nymphéas* or water lilies. In these paintings, the creative fire, before dying out, gave forth a final spark, igniting the imagination of future generations. They were a symbolic transmission of the flame in the creative relay race that is life.

Around 1900, when Monet started building his Giverny pond and garden, there was a profound revolution in thought. Henri Bergson, the great French philosopher, who died in 1941, led the revolt against materialism and related time and life in his "creative evolution." Einstein brought out his thought-shattering concepts of relativity based on a new use of light as a constant of the universe. The notion of time as an imperative of life suddenly took on new importance in man's consciousness. Marcel Proust tried in literature to recapture time already past. The camera and the cinema were changing man's vision, giving him the means to record and capture segments of time. In a curious way the impressionists previsioned the coming change.

Maybe painting should be re-evaluated and considered as one of the major thought-processes of humanity. The artist may through intuition see certain truths and unknowingly express them on a canvas; he may well be ahead of the scientists, writers, and philosophers of his time. Even the greatest scientists admit that in scientific discovery there is a part of intuition, of creative inspiration; they too are artists. The painters who discovered the visual properties of light changed the vision of the world and opened the eyes of scientists.

Einstein's conclusion that matter and energy are interchangeable terms curiously paralleled Monet's and the impressionists' research. These painters had for many years disintegrated on their canvases the tangible vision of nature; they were not painting the solidity, the substance of matter, but, by transcribing the color sensations that reached their eyes, unwittingly were making energy notations. For light is energy; color is a variation of light's energy.

Monet tried to "fix his sensations," the fleeting imprint on his eye. The painters of the period became living sensitized films, competing with the camera in the recording of nature. Light became the principal and unique subject of painting. Theirs was a daring gesture. They opened the door to all modern art. Once the apparent unity of visible nature was dislocated, light broken up into color components, once the questioning mind was focused onto that which had never been questioned, man's vision of the world could never again be the same.

Out of the impressionistic dogma of light split up into its components on the canvas and optically recomposed in the spectator's mind came the necessity to apply paint differently. The spectator, confronted by the seemingly loose, deliberately unprecise brushstrokes of Monet, by his transitory impressions of time fleeting on the surface of reality, has to contribute his share of participation. A painting never again would look photographically finished on the canvas; the ending had to be supplied by those who saw it. The demand for totally realistic art is an acknowledgment of mental laziness, a refusal of effort, and in the end a debasement of art and of the individual.

The Gestalt theory of perception had around 1910 discovered that the human mind tends to the act of closure; an unfinished, a suggested, circle looks to us still like a circle. The "unfinished," the incompletely defined canvases of Monet are the incompleted aspects of reality that still look to us like reality, and more so than the exact portrayal of nature by the realists. Even the great representational painters always left in their art an escape for the imagination; Rembrandt's escape hatch lay in the miracle of illuminated form losing itself in shadow.

Through the interstices between the rough brushstrokes of the impressionists, mystery could be sensed. For the painter seemed to say: This is all that can be portrayed, the rest cannot be portrayed. To define form completely, to describe all, "to finish," is to die.

The great painters knew that great secret and had the strength not to paint it. A Chinese sage said, "The greatest perfection / must appear imperfect, / Then it will be infinite / in its effect." One discovers how much a brushstroke is a true expression of the artist by studying the earliest works of the great painters. In a corner of one of these canvases there is always an area, seemingly unimportant, where a few brushstrokes become through the years the silent witnesses of the artist's inescapable nature. When, fifty or sixty years later, in the full possession of his creative means, the artist paints a picture, the small original pattern of brushstrokes, like a seed planted in fertile soil, has multiplied, and the whole new canvas bears a profound resemblance to the original imprint of personality.

The brush is but the extension of the artist's eye; as the needle of a seismograph shows the slightest tremors of the earth, so the brush-needle shows on the canvas the slightest tremors of the artist's emotions. To free his eye, to purify his vision, Monet attempted to disconnect his mind. Paul Valéry defines vision: "To see is to forget the names of the things one sees." Monet tried to connect in an inspired automatism the eye directly to the hand of the painter.

He painted with the suppleness of an artist who wanted a deep union with nature; his brushstrokes, his calligraphy, were a pliant reflection of his vision. In fact, Monet wrote, "I have no other wish than a close fusion with nature, and I desire no other fate than (according to Goethe's precept) to have worked and lived in harmony with her laws."

As an impressionist, Monet was always conscious of time. Vollard told this story to Degas: "Listen, Monsieur Degas . . . one day in Varengeville I saw a small car arrive in a cloud of dust. Monet gets out, looks at the sun, consults his watch, and says, 'I am half an hour late; I will come back tomorrow.'" Monet would choose a subject, then paint it for days, months, years under every hourly changing aspect of light, the succession of views creating a giant cinematographic color film. He returned at precise hours of the day, to be sure to see the subject under identical conditions, then put that canvas away to work on another that corresponded to the changing light. Time guided him when he started his series of paintings of cathedrals, of haystacks, and of water lilies. The need for series expresses an artist's knowledge that nothing can be wholly perceived and expressed in one experience.

Just as the Japanese *makimonos,* horizontal landscapes with figures painted on long rolls of silk, preceded our cinema in the unreeling of time, so Monet often changed the shape of conventional canvases into long, narrow rectangular canvases which cannot be comprehended in one all-embracing view. One has to read them as one reads a line of text. In his masterpiece, the immense panoramic panels of the water lilies, now in the Paris Orangerie Museum, he envelops the spectator, who becomes immersed in the *Nymphéas.*

If it were possible to record on film in chronological order all the paintings created by an artist during his lifetime, the whole creative life, when unreeled, would give us a life capsule. An artist's life is a succession of creative moments, each one marking a chronological development; his works of art become the exterior signs of inner growth. The painters themselves, when they date their paintings, mark the significant and inspired moments of their creative lives. To capture and record time a painter paints; paintings become the inscriptions on the memory of the world.

Cézanne's series of apples, his series of the Mont Sainte-Victoire, Monet's water lilies, cathedrals, and haystacks are the images of man's creative motion flowing around a fixed point of interest, nature. That fixed point rallies the scattered senses, intensifies the creative urge by channeling its drive. This withdrawal from all-surrounding life, with the exception of the particle through which revelation is sought, is a painter's meditation. The creating of art is the revelation of oneself through oneself. This sense of being part of a celestial and earthly harmony creates an urge to express it. This perception of the infinite, through creative meditation, is the inspiration of the artist.

NOTES ON THE ILLUSTRATIONS

Claude Monet. 1840–1926. Born, France.
Photographs taken in 1954.

10 Over-all view of Monet's Giverny. In the distance is the house; in front of it, the French flower garden that the great impressionist master painted often. The two garden worlds of Monet, his French garden and his most private Oriental water-lily garden with its extraordinary pond, are separated by a road and a railroad. The water lily, *nymphéa,* or lotus-flower, is sacred to the Buddhists, a symbol of "the deliverance of the soul through knowledge." Here in the lotus garden Monet, from 1899 until his death in 1926, pursued his great visual meditation in paint, the *Nymphéas* series.

11 A view of Monet's small studio in the house. On the walls, some of the mas-

ter's paintings; the steps to the right lead up to the dining room. His son Michel still sees that fresh flowers are arranged throughout the house.

12 The yellow dining room, its walls hung with Japanese prints. The influence of Japan is present in many ways at Giverny.

13 Monet's impressionist flower garden; to the right, his house.

14 A detail from one of the paintings in Monet's famous *Nymphéas* series. The brushstrokes are the artist's handwriting, transcribing the mysterious fuṣion of sky reflected in water.

15 Detail of water-lily pond, where Monet studied light on water.

BONNARD

Cézanne once said, "I could keep myself busy for months without moving from one spot, just by leaning now to the right, now to the left." Pierre Bonnard found worlds to paint in the personal, intimate world that surrounded him. His most radiant canvases were painted in the small, modest villa that stands in Le Cannet on top of a high hill dominating Cannes on the Mediterranean. There Pierre Bonnard lived from 1925 until his death in 1947.

When I went to Le Cannet in the middle of the summer, there were complete quiet and very little movement on the steeply winding avenues. In the haze, the red tile roofs of the carpetlike city below Bonnard's house combined with bright geraniums in a glimmering visual pattern. Then the pink walls of his villa were faded by sun and rain. A beautiful garden surrounded it, dense and thick; patterns of trees, shrubs, flowers, bushes intermingled, pierced with windowlike openings through which the eye escaped into a panorama of sky, mountains, sea, and distant Cannes.

On a clothes rack in the entrance hall hung the soft beach hat Bonnard loved to wear, the kind of hat a French bourgeois wore to the seashore in 1900. In its limp, amorphic shape one sensed the love of ease of the man who wore it. In the dining room that opened out onto a garden terrace still stood an immense table covered with a thick dull-red felt cloth, scattered with empty fruit baskets and jars. This red felt cloth was the singing accent in many of the Bonnard paintings.

I walked up one flight to his simple bedroom with its little open washbasin. The walls were pale blue; a narrow dust-gray bed stood next to the small window. Pale, worn remnants of clothing were still in their place—the formless sweaters and jackets of an elderly gentleman. Across the narrow hall there was a boudoir, and, beyond, Madame Bonnard's bedroom, where a yellow-painted wooden terrace opened out onto the trunks of palm trees and the immense blue of the Mediterranean. A torn Japanese print decorated the wall of the boudoir, a remnant of the late nineteenth century, when the Japanese influence was beginning to be felt.

His bedroom communicated with a bathroom, perhaps the most arresting room in Bonnard's house. For it was this simple white and blue tiled room with its antiquated gas water-heater, illuminated by intense sunlight and an immense luminous view, which gave him the background for many of the paintings of his greatest nudes. A white bathrobe hung in soft folds on one wall.

Not far from that room was his studio, the smallest studio of any great modern painter, a most impractical and uncomfortable workroom. In this already cramped area a tall platform had been erected. On it stood a couch, a work table, an armchair.

Bonnard used to tack to the walls the canvases on which he was working—several paintings would hang side by side. He worked on two or three at the same time, returning to add an accent after many days or even months. A slow accumulation of sensation was both Bonnard's life and method; he never knew where any canvas would stop. He cut off the canvas whenever he felt his emotional needs were satisfied.

There was no haste in the execution of his art. The brush seems to have meandered over the canvas as if the painter had time to pause and enjoy, and sensuously, caressingly describe.

On the wall above his shelves, right in the middle of his working area, he had neatly arranged and clearly exposed his inner admirations: Delacroix, Picasso, Vermeer, Monet, Seurat, Gauguin, classical Greek sculpture, and even a preferred Bonnard hung in a rich mixture of black and white and color reproductions. Three cheap colored postcards of the Midi gave life to a map of Cannes. Above it hung the strangest souvenirs of all—silver chocolate wrappings neatly pinned into various sizes and shapes. Glowing next to this museum, the crumpled, glistening tinfoil was a constant reminder of the master of all art, light. On some of the tinfoil there was a stamped pattern. It seemed to hold light captive. All his life Bonnard was fascinated by pattern.

The repeated forms of the wallpapers, the checkered tablecloths, the designs in fabrics of women's dresses, the patterns of leaves and flowers created a visual pattern that, like rhythm in music, gave a beat against which melody could sing. But pattern had another purpose: like a beat repeated or an incantation, it fascinated and hypnotized. A spell was cast on the spectator; one was snared and then one entered Bonnard's world. To achieve the true play of light, diamonds are cut; to keep light glowing on a canvas, Bonnard used many-faceted patterns that cut the surfaces of his paintings.

His art is a magnification of the modest. It was within his bourgeois surroundings that some of the most triumphant affirmations of the beauty of everyday existence were created. The dining room, the kitchen, the bath were stages for the observation of the everyday behavior of human beings, and his people live and behave in his paintings as though unobserved.

"Bonnard, one must beautify," said Renoir to his friend. There is the secret of art's universal appeal. Bonnard covered reality with his emotions, which he expressed through the infinite richness of his color. His was the same desire to adorn the object of one's love and admiration that made the primitives put precious stones and gold into religious paintings.

Out of his small gray, cell-like studio Bonnard's lyrical outburst of color was he triumphant song of a man in love, in love with art, in love with painting. Bonnard's art is a serenade of a man in love with life.

Bonnard was extremely timid. His simple and withdrawing nature never gave rise to the bold, egotistical aspirations of Cézanne or of most artists. He did not see himself as the founder of any school, never envisioned himself as another God re-creating his own universe in competition with the Creator. Nature dominated him because of his extreme susceptibility to the slightest pressure of impression. He once said he would rather keep flowers in a room separate from his studio while he was painting them so that they would not become overbearing. Antoinette, the woman who was his housekeeper for twenty years and who still kept the villa, said to me, "He liked my bouquets but he would never paint them right away. . . . He let the flowers wilt and then he started painting; he said that way they would have more presence."

A cautious approach, a bourgeois prudence, was Bonnard's way of life. Antoinette recalled how economical he was. He insisted on going over every detail of his household's accounts. The drawers of his desk were still filled with numerous receipts, laundry and electric bills, neat little notebooks in which he made lists of his expenses. He had studied first for the position of small *fonctionnaire* in the government recording-office which keeps track of births, deaths, and marriages; later he studied law. But by the time Bonnard was twenty-one he had abandoned his legal studies, and, fairly soon, in turn, the Ecole des Beaux-Arts.

He met Vuillard and Maurice Denis and the group of young painters who called themselves the *nabis,* after the Hebrew word for prophets. They were inspired by Gauguin, who preached of "the artist's right to dare everything," and were also influenced by Redon. Through Gauguin, Bonnard came under the influence of Japanese art and Japanese philosophy; he retained not only the graphic lessons but also the moral ones. From Zen Buddhism and other sources of Oriental thought, with which, like Redon, Bonnard seemed to have an inner rapport, he learned that the hard, the resistant is, in the end, vanquished by the soft, the pliant, much as rock is eroded by water.

The *nabis* explored new painting techniques in order to express more fully their personal feelings. They were, above all, painters for whom a painting was "essentially a flat surface covered with colors arranged in a certain order."

Cézanne's great discovery was that it was up to color to interpret light. Bonnard followed and enlarged on this theory; but where Cézanne's color is based on strict logic, on a severe and determined relationship to form, Bonnard's color is related to the senses. As Debussy broke rules of harmony to please his ear, so Bonnard broke rules of color to please his eye.

Like great musicians who have a perfect ear, Bonnard composed with a perfect eye. In his art the color-shape of a given area on a canvas is dictated not by the representation of an object in reality, but by the satisfaction of an eye-hunger for a certain color.

In his stressing of color and his abandonment of line, Bonnard is one of the greatest realists. For in nature there is no outline, only color and form. Line is an invention of the artist, a tool to convey his meaning. Bonnard used the interrelationship of massive areas of color to convey his meaning. His vision is the physical vision and not an intellectual translation of vision.

The impressionists painted in direct contact with nature; they transcribed literally what they saw. Bonnard made notation sketches, then painted from memory in the peace of his studio. From the distortions of memory comes the personal and original vision. His cropping of subject matter, the layout in the frame of his canvas, the scale of his subject matter, the intensity of his color were seldom ruled by logic or laws of perspective but obeyed the laws of his inner feelings as experienced through recollection.

In Proust, his contemporary, each minute, infinitely unimportant observation acquires significance through addition of facts and in the final picture fits in as a necessary, indispensable element; so in a Bonnard painting the smallest accent of light, the slightest touch of the brush, becomes indispensable to the final image of reality. This is a process of emotional accretion; and for the spectator the time spent by the eye in unraveling the accumulated tangle of colors, forms, and light becomes an experience of seemingly endless pleasure. This element of time-enjoyment in a painting is one of the greatest strengths of Bonnard's art.

And just as Proust coated the facts of everyday life with the endlessly subtle texture of the variations of his sensibility, so Bonnard coated his environment with the infinite subtlety of his color sensibility and the intricacy of his patterns. Bonnard used memory as Proust did; he painted all from memory, trying to recapture through tender recall the first inspiration, the first seduction, the first spark of love. Time for its own sake was not what Proust really sought. Time was a means, like a ladder descending into the depth of the past, a means to recapture the real object of his search, love.

In his essay, "On Love," Stendhal compared the process of love to a crystallization: "In the salt mines of Salzburg a bough stripped of its leaves by winter is thrown into the depths of the disused workings; two or three months later it is pulled out again, covered with brilliant crystals; even the tiniest twigs, no bigger than a tomtit's claw, are spangled with a vast number of shimmering, glittering diamonds, so that the original bough is no longer recognizable.

"I call crystallization that process of the mind which discovers fresh perfections in its beloved at every turn of events."

In love Stendhal never underestimated the visual process. We have two visions: one exterior, the other interior; one the vision of the eye, the other the vision of the mind or imagination.

The diamond crystals that transform the dead branch into an incandescent radiance need, in order to act fully on the beholder, the help of our two visions. Through imagination we adorn the glittering bough with unseen, unsuspected qualities, real only to our inner vision. Through the eye we receive the miracle of light glancing off the surfaces of the many-faceted crystals, breaking in prismatic beams through the crystalline formations, each new penetration and reflection seeming to add momentum to the original sunbeam before it strikes our eyes.

Bonnard took the reality and plunged it into the deep recesses of his mind, and there, through the accretion of sensation, through a literal falling in love with his subject, he endowed it with a new life. On the canvas a new crystallization took place; each brushstroke added particles of paint that, like the crystals on the bough, made each object painted an idealization of nature through light, and each painting an act of love.

The tenderness of his art does not make Bonnard a weak artist. It is as if his weakness reached such monumental proportions that it became strength. A Bonnard canvas is like a minute section of an impressionist painting enlarged X times. This physical magnification gives scale and grandeur, but it is also an emotional increase. His painting is a poster of the subtle; it shouts in a soft voice; it advertises privacy. He had retained from his early days, when he painted posters, the ability to dramatize the essentials. Later in his art the essentials became the hitherto unadvertised, the never before violently expressed moments of intimate tenderness.

Bonnard, in his rare comments on art, often used the word "seduction," and it is a key word in describing his art. For seduction is an emotional attraction, an unreasoning surrender to an impulse to admire, to find beauty, to possess; in fact, seduction is the first instant in the process of love.

For centuries a symbol of love in painting has been woman. And just as there are many aspects of love, there are many ways of portraying woman. Woman is present in almost all Bonnard paintings: either she is directly represented, a portrait or a nude; or she is glimpsed from the corner of the eye, present but seemingly absent in a family scene; or, as in the interiors or still lifes, her hand is felt in the arrangement of things. She is the mother nature of the interior, rearranging the nature that is her home.

Bonnard's art is a sublimation, a distillation. When he painted nudes, they were never the portrayal of flesh for its own sake. He painted a nude as chastely as if it were a flower.

This uninhibited intimacy with all that is beautiful and joy-giving is the key and fascination of Bonnard's art. When he painted the privacy of life, the everyday casual clutter, he was describing the core of family life.

This is what life with love looks like. The original crystals of seduction become the everyday objects of the home, laden with emotional associations. The coffeepot, the plate, the tablecloth become under his brush, as the *madeleine* under Proust's tongue, the sentimental, memory-evoking talismans.

For Bonnard, woman, and her portrayal, was one of the essentials of his art. But where most painters used the nude for decorative, sensuous effect, Bonnard invented a new vision of the female body. Each painting is an addition of knowledge that slowly, delicately, chastely brings us into a private world.

For the backgrounds of many of his nudes, he chose the bath, for this was the ultimate vision of privacy, the one place where in our civilization human beings are really natural, for they are unobserved, not on the defensive. For Degas, a woman washing was critically observed. The opinion of the artist is present in his art. For Bonnard, there was tender acceptance and no criticism.

His women wash, bathe, and move as if unobserved in that supreme, defenseless moment when all shame disappears because, through love, confidence and trust are born. His women know that they are loved and that the painter, like a lover, will adorn them in whatever instant he sees them with the all-embellishing magic of his crystallization. Bonnard expressed the peace, the trust, that reigns in the home. So happy and intimate and close had been his life with Madame Bonnard, the model of many of his canvases, that when she died in 1940 he could not bear his solitude. This need for the presence of love is the indispensable climate for a serene creation. Only the human beings who have known the true meaning of love mutually shared can express true joy. When we look at a Bonnard canvas its secret power is that healthy knowledge, that certitude that love can and does exist, and that man can find happiness and joy through love.

The austere simplicity of Bonnard's life, the bare whitewashed studio, like a monk's cell, the gentleness of his art, the tender originality of his color, and his all-enriching vision bring to mind the life and work of another painter of joy Fra Angelico. The Florentine monk centuries earlier had entranced the world with his ineffable visions. The rigid monastic discipline, the strict laws of Catholic dogma not only did not prevent, but, on the contrary, stimulated the creative out let; his art brimmed full with pure visual happiness. So Bonnard, centuries later, sheltered and concentrating his vision on the intimate, private world around him, invested it with magic richness.

NOTES ON THE ILLUSTRATIONS

Pierre Bonnard. 1867–1947. Born, France.
Photographs taken in 1955.

16 *The Breakfast Room*, 1930–1931. Oil, 63¼" × 44⅛". The Museum of Modern Art, New York.

17 The interior of Bonnard's studio in his small villa at Le Cannet behind Cannes, where he lived and painted from 1925 until his death in 1947. The studio, compared with the studios of other painters, is incredibly small, but here Bonnard was able to paint some of his largest canvases. The curious platform, protected by a railing, seems to reduce the space even more. In the foreground, his brushes and paints, just as he left them. On the back wall is a unique revelation, Bonnard's private admirations.

18 Bonnard's private artistic admirations. This wall in his studio is one of the most revealing documents of a great painter's inner thoughts that I have ever seen. It is like a small altar to the gods of his life, the presences he wanted near him. Reproductions of works by Picasso, Vermeer, Monet, Seurat, Gauguin, Bonnard himself, and Greek sculpture hang next to a map of Cannes and some chromo postcards. The crinkled chocolate papers neatly pinned and preserved enabled him to study the miracle of light, one of his lifetime preoccupations.

19 The bathroom of the villa at Le Cannet. Bonnard explored the intimacy of life further than any of his contemporaries. Dreary everyday reality was transformed by his art into an object of admiration and beauty. The folds of his bathrobe, as he left it, have the nobility of medieval sculpture.

20 *Nude with Lamp*, 1912. Oil, 29½" × 29½". Collection Hahnloser, Winterthur.

CÉZANNE 1

CÉZANNE 2

CÉZANNE

RENOIR 7

9
8

RENOIR

MONET 10

MONET

14

15

BONNARD

17

BONNARD 18

19

BONNARD

II

THE FAUVE GENERATION

MATISSE   ROUAULT   DERAIN   VLAMINCK   DUFY   VAN DONGEN

MATISSE

The case of Matisse is extraordinary. At seventy-one, an age when most people feel they have completed their life's work, he was stricken by disease. Until his death in 1954, he lived in a permanent state of convalescence. Yet, a miracle of will-power, he forced into his last fourteen years a splendid succession of achievements.

"Imagine an artist who would be spiritually in a permanent state of convalescence," Baudelaire wrote in his essay on Constantin Guys. "Convalescence is like a descent into childhood. The convalescent, like a child, enjoys to the limit the ability to be intensely interested in things. . . . The child sees everything as new. . . . Genius is but childhood recovered at will."

During the years of his illness Matisse never revealed a morbid thought in his work. The more he suffered, the more he withdrew from active life, the more he dared in his art. He did not confine himself to any single period or style. He evolved. And this capacity to evolve, to adapt oneself to change, is the gift of the child as well as of the artist.

Many great artists have led very long lives. Perhaps old age offers an opportunity to throw off the yoke of adulthood and, in a new yet final childhood, reinherit the unbridled creative wonder of youth. Matisse, in his old age, worked with the vitality of youth and the wisdom and knowledge of age.

In his last works, in his *papiers découpés,* in his paintings, in his book illustrations, in his chapel at Vence, he risked more than ever before. This was the courage of an old man, a genius who knew that he would soon die and who had everything to gain in exploring the preoccupations of his whole life—color and line.

After the Second World War, when I first visited Matisse in Paris, he lived on the Boulevard Montparnasse, a few hundred yards from the intersection of Boulevard Raspail. Between two wars Montparnasse had triumphed over Montmartre; nearby were the great meeting places, the cafés of La Rotonde, La Coupole, and Le Dôme.

A small self-service elevator took me to the sixth floor of a modern apartment house. When I was admitted I entered a long hall with several glass doors covered by curtains. In the studio, the living room of a conventional apartment, the light was so intense that the metal shutters had been drawn. A sensuous backdrop of many nudes dominated the room. In one corner stood a classical Greek torso of a woman, in another a large Polynesian polychrome figure, and near the win-

21 **MATISSE**   55

dows were his own sculptures, dark, shiny bronzes silhouetted against the light. On a chest of drawers rested many books. I noticed John Dewey's *Art as Experience,* and volumes on Cézanne, El Greco, the drawings of Leonardo da Vinci, and Chinese calligraphy. Hanging on the walls were Matisse's most recent canvases, vigorous, vital, and young. The room vibrated with the charge of color. Next to this intensely luminous studio was Matisse's bedroom, a smaller, darker room into which he could withdraw. Then, when refreshed, he would return to the light.

Wherever he was, life was reduced to one purpose—Matisse's creativeness. Everything was so arranged that his slightest desire, his slightest urge for expression, could be easily set into action. Illness became a justified excuse for eliminating all unnecessary activity. To protect him, as many of the problems of life as possible were solved in advance. How many creative people have yearned for fate to force them to concentrate upon only the problems they want to solve?

His protective shield from disturbances and interruptions of daily life was Madame Lydia Delectorskaya. A slight, blond, thin-lipped Russian woman, she was his nurse, housekeeper, secretary, companion, and model. With deep respect and obedience to the master, she satisfied his least desire with quiet efficiency. As I looked around the living room, she entered and announced that I could visit Matisse.

In the semidarkness of his bedroom I saw walls covered with drawings, studies in line, in bold black ink, of nudes and faces, and still lifes. Then, as I grew accustomed to the dark, I distinguished an old man lying in bed. He was extremely pale. The sheets, his face, his pajamas, the covering on the bed, all seemed bathed in the same yellow-white grayish mist.

This impression of softness was pierced by the sharp accents of light hitting the rims of his metal spectacles, hitting the thistles of hair that were his beard. The white beard, neatly clipped in a circular shape, gave an extra dimension to the face. The bald head and the round lenses of his glasses continued the circular movement. Only the perpendicular and the horizontal of the nose and mouth relieved the curvilinear mask.

His was no ordinary beard. It had been trimmed and shaped with a profound knowledge of form. It was more than a beard; it was a form fashioned in relation to other forms. As a smile appeared, the bristles moved and intelligent eyes showed behind the rims of his glasses. Those eyes were haunting. Small, in relation to the enlarged features of the face, they were magnetic in their grip. They penetrated, even intimidated. They were the eyes of a bird. As very old people sometimes do, he viewed with discernment all outside manifestations—a knowing, questioning, quizzical appraisal. In a voice that was low and soft he greeted me.

Because I wanted to photograph him, he got out of bed. I returned to the living room. He entered, impeccably dressed in brown trousers and a loose beige jacket. He sat down in an armchair, his legs assuming, as they crossed, the pose for a formal portrait. There was an extraordinary grandeur in his bearing. He sat like a king, patient and purposely severe. Of all the painters I have seen, Matisse was by far the most awesome; physically and emotionally he kept his distance. Later Madame Lydia said, "He hates to see himself smiling in a picture." Somehow, his voice seemed weak in contrast to the monumental stature of his appearance. As he posed I said that he reminded me of a Venetian portrait. "Yes," he said with a smile, "I'm an old *sbire revêche*" (literally, a severe myrmidon).

But aloofness and reserve seemed a self-imposed discipline on a tender, emotional nature. In him intelligence, culture, and wisdom blended with caustic French irony and doubt. Not self-doubt—there was none of that—but a doubt or *méfiance* of everything outside of himself. He was steady and precise, demanding that each term be carefully defined. The precision and logic of French education were perceptible in his speech. His scientific analysis of light, his careful movement of pieces of paper, his numerous preparatory sketches, were cautious steps before any definite or final commitment.

When, because of illness, it became difficult for him to move or to stand before an easel, he solved these problems in an intelligent and systematic way. For instance, he had sheets of paper painted to match his colors. By cutting and pasting these papers he created striking designs, collages, or, exactly, *papiers découpés.*

Matisse, unlike the cubists, did not use collage as an end in itself. It was a method to facilitate his experiments. Earlier cubist collages by Braque and Picasso are predominantly brown and gray; Matisse—in his own words—"sculpted with color." With scissors he cut paper in the way that a sculptor with his chisel cuts into stone. On a colored background, these papers were rearranged many times, held with pins until he was satisfied with the design, then secured with glue. These bold compositions came closer to abstraction than any of his other works. Here were Matisse the sculptor and Matisse the painter wedded in a new medium.

In retrospect, *papiers découpés* may well be his greatest contribution to twentieth-century art. As experiments they are in step with modern research in pure color in art, in electronics, in films. Matisse said, "The future of art is in light." His play with color sensations was bolder than that of any artist before him.

His experiments led him one logical step further, to the deeper problem of light itself. Now he could sculpt with color through light. In the stained-glass windows of the chapel at Vence he culminated a lifetime of research in color and light.

To test his theories, he transformed his immense apartment in Cimiez, above Nice, into a scale model of the future chapel. The windows were high, the ceilings lofty. From the ornate balcony, so familiar in Matisse's early Riviera paintings, he could see the tops of palm trees swishing in the summer breeze. Beyond lay the roofs of Nice, then the scintillating blue sea. This view, however, was no longer the principal source of his inspiration.

Pasted on a white wall was an imaginary window, a window created out of colored paper. One of the actual windows of the room was half covered by the same pattern in samples of colored glass. As the room could be darkened, Matisse was able to put sheets of white paper in front of the stained glass to work out his theory of complementary light. In balancing primary colors, blue and yellow, with green, he found that the resulting light created within the white box of the chapel would be rose violet. Matisse was attempting to advance beyond painting, by imprinting on the senses of the spectator colors that did not exist in reality but only in the mind.

In another room at Cimiez, his "drawing research center," the ceiling, the walls, everything was white, the whole room bathed in light. Across one wall was stretched a large sheet of loosely pinned paper on which he had drawn in charcoal the Virgin and Child. Standing briefly during his working hours, with a piece of charcoal attached to a long stick, he drew with one hand, as he had drawn earlier in 1931 the figures of *The Dance* in the great collection of the Barnes Foundation in Merion, Pennsylvania. The sureness of his hand and of his conception was incredible, the reward of constant practice. For Matisse, obsessed with line, this was the apotheosis of a whole lifetime of draftsmanship.

The drawing was the most glorious I had ever seen. Its unexpected scale, twenty by thirty feet, made one physically penetrate into it. Usually sketches for murals are small notations, and one has to imagine them in their actual size. Here, instead, hung a sketch that was both a project and a finished work of art. The Virgin, at that stage, was in a robe made of stars; the sky behind her was studded with stars that looked like the petals of flowers. The head of the Child was another breast on the Mother's body. Resplendent, splendid, the drawing was a chant of intellectual fervor expressed through the artist's inventiveness.

Opposite was another immense mural, equally large, representing the Stations of the Cross. The Stations were still in a tentative state, faintly indicated in light charcoal. Many of the lines had been erased. The unnecessary eliminated, emotion was reduced to the essential moment. This series of drawings of Christ's agony was the only manifestation of suffering that I have ever seen in any of Matisse's work. He would portray tragedy only in the presence of God; never did he expose his emotions to the art buyers of the world. Proud, civilized, and sensitive, he wanted his art to celebrate his faith that a profound life could be a happy life. More than any other modern painter, Matisse expressed that particularly French appreciation of *joie de vivre*.

As an intelligent Frenchman, Matisse tried to discipline his sensuousness into order, into form. He had a classical desire to restrain the emotions. His was the world of the highest senses, a world of *jouissance,* of pleasure stronger than enjoyment. In his art, the seemingly superficial, pretty side of life is raised to another level. He made the pretty beautiful, conferring nobility on charm.

Naturally, woman was his principal subject; he surrounded her with ornaments —fruits, flowers, plumes, birds, rare fabrics—all to enhance seduction. She is the promise of happiness—as Baudelaire wrote, "a divinity, a star, who presides at all the conceptions of the male brain." The image of the artist as a lover creating himself the object of his love contributes to the art of Matisse a male vigor.

One must read Baudelaire, for his influence on the thinking of French artists in general and on Matisse in particular was profound. The poet of intellectual escape, he was able to transform visions into sensual form. *Luxe, Calme, et Volupté,* the title of one of Matisse's great compositions, was taken from Baudelaire's poem, "L'Invitation au Voyage." In every cultivated Frenchman there is a longing for liberation, a desire to break the conventions of the *bourgeoisie.* Baudelaire's invitation to discovery is the key to the quest of the artist. And, with escape, with adventure, there is usually the association of love.

The exotic spell of the Orient has awakened many writers, poets, painters to new visual stimulations. Ingres with his odalisques and *Bain Turc* brought the voluptuous Orient to conventional France. Then Delacroix, the master of color, was transformed by his experiences in North Africa. Nearly a century later, Matisse followed Delacroix's footsteps, and in Matisse's art the rich influence of Mohammedan or Islamic art found its fullest flowering. The nineteenth century had been stamped by the revelations of Ingres and Delacroix. The twentieth saw Matisse take possession of the Afro-Islamic motif. So strong was Matisse's hold that few artists dared touch his domain. Only after his death could the odalisque and the Moorish interior be approached by other painters.

In his long life Matisse had perhaps traveled more than any other great painter. North Africa, America, Russia, Tahiti, Spain, Germany, England, Italy, Scandinavia, Holland, many other places came under the scrutiny of his hungry eyes.

As one reads Matisse's extraordinarily perceptive biography by Alfred H. Barr, Jr., one is struck by the sequences of dates, places, and events which seem to fit into a unique pattern. They offer clues to a perhaps insufficiently stressed aspect of the thinking of a great artist. Is it possible to find a unifying thread that, unknown to Matisse himself, was the secret motivation of his creative life? Man has the power of synthesis, of welding together the lessons of centuries of diverse cultures. From this unity the genius can spring forth to new and as yet unexplained visions.

As early as 1905 Matisse worked in Collioure, ten miles from the border of Spain, and, as late as 1492, a Moorish stronghold. Matisse went to Africa for the first time in 1906, and we know that in Berlin in 1910 the great Islamic exhibition created a lasting impression on him.

What, briefly, in Mohammedan art played such a powerful role in Matisse's life? The origin is in Persia, from where it wandered far into India, China, and Europe. Centuries later, under the stimulation of Byzantine and Islamic art, memory images of Persian art, dormant in the deep subconscious of European cultures, were reactivated. The impact and the enthusiasm with which the Islamic influences were received was in reality the joy of recognition. Perhaps not enough has yet been said about the role Islamic culture has played in European art. And, in the twentieth century, it is important to remember that Mohammed, in his fear of idolatry, forbade the representation of the human form. Thus for centuries Mohammedan art relied on pattern and ornament, in one word, abstraction, for its principal inspiration.

Here we touch on the fascinating adventure of modern art. What has seemed for so long a freak of destiny, the fact that advanced French painting was first understood by faraway Russians, can perhaps be explained by the influence of Islam.

The discovery of abstract art is generally attributed to Kandinsky, a Russian of Siberian origin. The culture of Russia has been forever branded by the visual splendor of Christian Byzantium and of Mohammedan Islam. Byzantine ornament and Islamic abstraction are imprinted on Russian cultural memory. With this in mind, it may seem less surprising that Shchukin, the Russian merchant, was the first great patron of Matisse. He found instinctively in Matisse's art a resonance with this yearning for Oriental splendor.

The same Russians who discovered Matisse discovered also Picasso, who received Islamic influences through his native Spain. Before him Cézanne, the father of modern art—again first appreciated by Russian collectors—surely had been subtly inoculated with the abstract precepts of Islam. His native Aix lay close to Spain. North Africa was just across the Mediterranean. And, through his admiration for El Greco, some of the tragic mystery of Islam may also have penetrated his sensitivity.

To the eyes of the Russians, the rich and vibrant color patterns of Matisse brought emotional satisfaction. His sun-drenched canvases were like glowing suns. They were windows to the south.

Matisse was the first *fauve,* maybe because he was the first to understand the lesson of the southern sun, the lesson of Cézanne, that form is at its maximum when color is at its maximum. Matisse knew that the sun, the source of light, can be transcribed in painting only through the equivalence of color. It is impossible to match its brightness, but through the vividness of hue our eyes can receive a stimulation similar, if not equal, to intense illumination. To intensity of color, Matisse added the power of line. He made color inseparable from line. In his art, line is the fluid frontier of color sensation.

Matisse himself found in sun-conditioned Islamic thought the nourishment for his inspiration. In early Moslem ornaments, the twist of the tendrils of the vine is the main source of inspiration. This symbolic unfolding, this groping search of the vine was used by the Arab scribes in their rounded script. Matisse, in his yearning to express the power of life, repeatedly used the curvilinear shapes of leaves and the sinuous forms of female bodies to stress the unity of nature. The line that delineates his nudes, the line that describes objects and their interrelationships, is the line that ties all together, to allow the spectator to comprehend in one swoop the undulating unity of the universe. The rubber plant leaves that Matisse scissored out of colored papers rejoin in their basic shapes the shapes of his nudes. Nature is one. As in Cézanne's paintings of bathers there is no division between man and his surroundings.

For Matisse, the Mohammedan emphasis on calligraphic as opposed to representational images became a source of fascinating study. When he created his great book of *papiers découpés, Jazz,* he wrote out in longhand the whole text. In the same way, a few years later, he also transcribed in his own hand the poems of Charles d'Orléans, another example of his effort to restore to written images their long abandoned prestige.

Arabic writing, like Chinese and Japanese calligraphy, expresses more than just the meaning of words. The flowing rhythmic scripts seem to imitate the basic rhythms of life. In his greatest canvases, Matisse tried to express through the movement of the nude human body rhythms that are also the signs of the beat of life. His famous composition, *The Dance,* first commissioned by Shchukin and reinterpreted in the Barnes murals, offers in its vital arabesques a graphic translation of rhythm through the movement of the body.

Rhythm, beat, life were essential to Matisse. His vitality is expressed through the visual exuberance, the ornamental richness of his art. For Matisse the decorative was not the superfluous, but the abundance of life's creativity. In his paintings the flowered shawls, the patterned tiles, the flowered wallpapers assume the value of symbols of the artist's energy.

He believed in lavishing the gift of the artist. The eye loses itself quickly in the infinite repetition of patterns, just as the eye, when contemplating the uncountable multitude of stars, leads the mind to a notion of infinity. This pleasurable, even hypnotic, power of ornament has been knowingly used by Matisse, who in his art sought to give a sensation of rest, of peace. He said, "What I dream of is an art of balance, of purity and serenity devoid of trouble and depressing subject matter. An art which might be for every mental worker, be he businessman or writer, like an appeasing influence, like a mental soother, something like a good armchair in which to rest from physical fatigue." A Matisse painting is like a *riad*, a visual oasis and a glimpse of paradise on earth. It is not a coincidence that the North African house was turned toward an inner garden, the *riad*, in which man could seek joy and repose.

When Matisse through the magic of his art created the momentary but incessantly recurrent sensation of joy and beauty, he was allowing us to escape reality. His ability to entice us from everyday life, as if under a charmed spell, reveals much about himself. His travels, his need for the transformation of reality—even by the use of disguise—his yearning for the exotic, his search for beauty were the ambitious and silent cries of a great artist who undauntedly believed in the grandeur of a beauty that he instinctively knew he could reveal through his art. And when, toward the end of his life, he built a chapel, he sought to create the image of his ideal place, where man could be cleansed by his surroundings, and then, when visually purified, could come before God unsullied.

The chapel at Vence, with its tiles, with its green and yellow and blue stained-glass windows that make one believe that a sunlit garden is surrounding the pure white walls, is a spiritual *riad*. The door to the confessional, fabulously chiseled from wood and rubbed with white, is like the rarest ornament of a mosque. The black line drawings on the white tile walls are the calligraphy of Matisse's faith. This chapel is his testament. In its color, light, and line, Matisse's lifelong quest for a place of rest and peace combined in a final daring masterpiece. The unity that he achieved, the peace that he found, were again the tangible expression of his fervent belief in the unity of the world. To this chapel he brought the experience of many cultures. This final unification of all creative faiths was Matisse's supreme homage to the creator of all.

NOTES ON THE ILLUSTRATIONS

Henri Matisse. 1869–1954. Born, France.
Photographs taken in 1949, 1951.

21 Henri Matisse caught in a rare smiling mood, in the living-room studio of his Paris apartment.

22 *Lemons against a fleur-de-lis background,* 1943. Oil, 19¾" × 25¾". Collection Miss Loula Lasker, New York.

23 The view from the altar of the Vence Chapel. On the rear wall, the stations of the cross painted in black on glazed tiles. On the left corner of the Virgin

and Child composition is the carved wood door of the confessional. On the right, the yellow, green, and blue stained-glass windows. The studied result of Matisse's light is that the all white walls take on a mauve-pink optical hue. The richest effect is the deep purple hue seen through the openings of the carved, lacelike confessional door. This chapel is Matisse's masterpiece, his message to the artists of the future; line is used as a stenography of communication, color used separately from form and line.

24 An early study for the Virgin and Child, drawn full scale in Matisse's studio in Nice. For these gigantic drawings Matisse used charcoal attached to a long stick.

25 In the Cimiez apartment above Nice, Matisse's working table as it looked when he was planning the chapel: a charcoal sketch for the stations of the cross; a charcoal study of a head; a scaled doll of a Dominican nun dressed in the black and white of her order. On the cardboard model of the chapel Matisse previsioned the finished effects of his orchestration of light, line, space, and architecture. In the background, the tall, narrow yellow, green, and blue paper cutouts prefigured the stained glass.

26 In the finished chapel the stained-glass windows of the choir filter light mysteriously. In the foreground, the altar with the crucifix and the candle sticks designed by Matisse.

27 Detail in the studio, the original plaster of the 1907 *Reclining Nude* against the fabulous backdrop of his own painted tiles, exotic fabric, and Japanese pottery. These were early sources of inspiration to Matisse and represent his permanent need of the stimulation of visual patterns.

28 A. Paris: In 1951 Matisse in the living room of his Boulevard Montparnasse apartment, at work on his design for the dust jacket of Alfred H. Barr, Jr.'s *Matisse: His Art and Public.*
B. Paris: On the wall, a Matisse painting and a plate ready for etching. On the commode, art books and a head, *Jeannette I,* 1910.
C. Paris: A Polynesian sculpture, an early Matisse, and his design of intense color in pasted paper for a stained-glass window, and an aquatint in black and white which had just returned from the printer's.
D. Paris: Matisse speaking.
E. Nice: Under a Chinese calligraphy plaque stand a Japanese jar, Persian brass, two figures from Bambara, and, on the right, two folk-art jugs.
F. Nice: View from the studio.
G. Nice: Maquette in glass of a section of a chapel window.
H. Paris: Matisse gestures.
I. Nice: Two palettes.
J. Paris: Sculptures on the window sill.
K. Paris: Matisse in a discussion.
L. Nice: In a vitrine, a Bakuba headmask from Africa.

29 In the Paris studio-living room, a bright-colored couch; on the wall, *Gray Nude,* 1929; by the window, the bronze *Jeannette IV.*

30 *The Hindu Pose,* 1923. Oil, 28½" × 23⅜". Collection Mr. and Mrs. Donald S. Stralem, New York.

ROUAULT

In the doorway of a dimly lit living room appeared a man with an extraordinary lunar face. His complexion was pale, his stare fixed, with eyelids blinking quickly over large pale blue eyes. There were yellow streaks on his eyelids, as though while painting he had rubbed his eyes, smearing some yellow pigment. The wrinkles on his face were thin, like the lines on a sensitive young hand. The wide mouth with its thick lips covered a row of widely spaced, protruding yellow teeth. He was dressed in a light bluish-gray suit, a stiff white collar, and a large knotted tie fixed with a ceremonial pin. And, in the intimacy of his own home, he wore a hat, a formal gray Homburg. This was "Monsieur Rouault," the master on an official appearance.

At the threshold of the room Georges Rouault stopped and stood still, as if enjoying the effect of his entrance. His daughter produced a stenotyping machine and hid in a corner to take down every word her father was about to say. Her straight hair, parted in the middle, was pulled tight. Her face, slightly tilted to one side, bore the wan smile of a woman used to being browbeaten.

The living-room furniture was dark, Gothic. In an enormous cupboard opposite a sideboard open shelves displayed decorated porcelain plates. Near the window were a lectern, a wooden eagle with wings outstretched, an armchair worthy of an archbishop. The dark wood, the scale of the objects, crowded the small conventional room. The window, hung with lace curtains, opened onto an extraordinary cacophony of a station square. Milling in front of the Gare de Lyon, the busiest railway station in Paris, were hundreds of taxis, buses, bicycles, porters, trucks.

Rouault moved slowly. He sat down and began a monologue addressed mostly to himself. My questions, like a tap, released a long stream of recollection. He had much to tell, but age jumbled the chronology in his memory. It was extraordinary to be in the presence of someone who spoke of Degas, of Cézanne, and of Renoir—as his contemporaries: "I looked at Cézanne's canvas and said . . ."; "Cézanne said to me . . ." Elaborate recollections followed; he played the record of his memory regardless of his audience.

He was often bitter. He said that for many years Ambroise Vollard, the famous art dealer, used him as his secret advisor. He seldom bought a painting without consulting Rouault. Rouault felt he was the art director behind the scenes, and this unacknowledged role had left its scar. At a time when Rouault's own art was not sufficiently appreciated, he found himself employed to evaluate other people's productions. Vollard also kept him working day and night on illustrations, with no time for life. He was always kept busy changing, correcting, never ready. He seemed bitter that the Germans and the Russians and the Americans had appreciated his art and discovered him before his own compatriots. He was bitter that success had come so late in his life—too late for him to enjoy. Only when Rouault was over seventy could he afford to go to Venice.

"You know," he said, "I have never got on with officials . . . they have cared little for me. They've let me be in my little nook. And now that I'm half dead they have tried to come and fetch me.

"Isn't that so, Isabelle?" He turned to his daughter. "They waited until I was old and feeble to propose me for a seat in the Institute. You can guess I sent them away with their tails between their legs, eh? They've waited for me to be nearly dead to come to fetch me."

Funny, agile gestures of his hands illustrated his stories and reminded me of the accents and mimicry of a Punch-and-Judy show. He acted out a role. His stylized movements performed a carefully rehearsed pantomime. He lowered his head and raised his arms when sadness was his mood. He raised his head and stretched his arms wide for joy. To display cunning he scratched and curled his body.

An understanding of the theatrical gesture is a key to Rouault's art as well as to his conversation. Many artists have this gift for mimicry, which is part of the ability to observe and, after having observed, to draw. The artist must be able to imitate, to project himself inside whatever he wants to draw. This is why Rouault drew with such ferocity and understanding and humor the soldier, the prostitute, the judge, the lawyer; he could act out all parts in his own *commedia dell'arte*. He was both its actor and playwright.

Present in all of his stories and gestures was laughter, violent, cruel, and sardonic. When the thick lips of his wide mouth stretched into a grin, his yellow teeth protruded. When he looked over the photographs of himself he chose the one of himself laughing violently, making a strong gesture with his hand.

"I am fed up with always seeming sad and tragic," he said. "I am not. I like a good laughing picture of myself."

Rouault liked to laugh. But it was a satirical, Rabelaisian laugh. This mystic, this man who had been all his life preoccupied with religion, had the rough humor of a country priest. And in Rouault one understood how close laughter is to tragedy.

Rouault never outlived the 1900s. In his talk he tangled turn-of-the-century political intrigues with his admiration for Albert Besnard, a French *pompier* academician, his admiration for his Beaux-Arts teacher Gustave Moreau, his admiration for everthing in a past era. He never mentioned any contemporary artist except Matisse.

Of all the twentieth-century painters, Matisse was Rouault's oldest friend. Although the two men—both ill—did not see each other often, their friendship remained. The link between them was Gustave Moreau, under whom they had studied at the Beaux-Arts. Moreau, who painted mythological scenes in the style of the 1890s—pictures of Salomé in luminous glazes and small jewel-like touches of color—was preoccupied with texture, sensuousness, the voluptuous richness of precious stones. His lessons are still felt in both Matisse's and Rouault's work. And his students, these two geniuses, met toward the end of their lives in the same preoccupation with religion, the same interest in the stained-glass medium.

There seemed to be no contact between Rouault and his surroundings. Considered one of the leaders of the modern school, he took a stand against everything modern. He believed that since the days of his early manhood people had forgotten how to draw, how to paint. He felt that too many of his contemporaries had been by-passed and not sufficiently appreciated.

"All these youngsters think they can build on emptiness," he said. "Nothing emerges from nothing. You must be humble and not think that you know. Everything must be begun again . . . and I who have waited until seventy to go to Italy!"

While Rouault talked, I looked at his feet. Although carefully and so formally attired, he wore felt bedroom slippers. This was a telltale evidence that he lived an old man's life and perhaps was more of an invalid than he appeared. He gave the impression of an animal in a cage. One felt that Rouault was suffocating and lacked the vigor, because of age, to break his chains, and that whatever energy remained he poured into his violent canvases. The sad house, the sad, dull apartment, were out of scale with the giant's soul. As he talked, some of his gestures reminded one of Michelangelo's prophets. There were flashes of extraordinary grandeur in his speech and gesture that contradicted the pettiness of what he said.

But old as he was, he remained master of his house. One felt a fear of disturbing the great old man in the manner in which his daughter spoke to him. As I left, Mademoiselle Rouault grasped my hand and said, "Thank you for your discretion." Modesty, withdrawal seemed to be the keynote of that disciplined life in which a tormented, violent human being poured his passion into painting. It was striking that in the presence of a great religious painter never were the words "God" or "religion" or "faith" mentioned. Religion seemed to be a deeply hidden inner self in Rouault which he revealed only through his art.

Some years later I returned for a second visit with Rouault. I stood again in the dark living room. It was impossible to see his studio. Few had ever been allowed in it, or to see him "cook" at his painting. This time, through the white doors, appeared a white ghost. Rouault was dressed all in white—a white surgeon's coat tied with a simple belt, a white surgeon's cap on his head. This was his working costume. And he wore eyeglasses rimmed with plastic—incongruously modern in the medieval setting of his apartment.

In his right hand he held a huge, curved, carefully scraped palette, the traditional palette of the Beaux-Arts student, a bottle of turpentine, an inexplicable aluminum funnel, a jar with a few brushes. Much thinner than before, he looked younger and more ethereal. With the same absent-minded grandeur in his manner he started again on his stream of recollections. However, there were less fire, fewer gestures when he spoke. His daughter brought in one of his latest paintings; it was an exciting, dynamic canvas charged with every ounce of energy that remained in Rouault's body. The canvas was yellow-green. The scraped paint on Rouault's palette was yellow-green. This was the light that Rouault saw in his old age, the same light that seemed to surround Matisse in the Vence windows. Was there a mysterious relationship between these men's old age and their desire for the warmth of sun color?

In many of Rouault's late canvases a sun or a moon is the source of all light, a golden haze which spills over from the canvas onto the frame. It is more than just the light that concerns every painter. There is a mysticism in the light, as though the preoccupation with light had led this man away from this planet into another world. Rouault and Matisse seemed to have gone beyond the material on this planet. They went beyond matter to the source of all life and of all painting, this thing that we call "sun" and beyond which is God. Rouault and Matisse reached their mysticism not through form but through light.

In the golden radiance which bathes his last works, Rouault seemed to have glimpsed the light of the Promised Land—that short, stocky, great man with the clown's face and the gestures of a prophet, with the sad mouth and the blinking eyes, who stood high above the turmoil of the street, oblivious to its whistles, klaxons, shouts, and crowds.

NOTES ON THE ILLUSTRATIONS

Georges Rouault. 1871–1958. Born, France.
Photographs taken in 1950, 1953, 1956.

31 *The Old Clown*. Oil. Collection Stavros Niarchos.

32 A sequence of Rouault acting out his conversation.

33 Rouault carried away by his vision.

34 His Paris living room with its dark Gothic furniture, a lectern, and a crucifix decorated by Rouault.

35 A painted plate and oiled papers that Rouault used to press against his still wet painting to enrich texture.

36 "He was oppressed, and was afflicted,
Yet he opened not his mouth."
Plate from *Miserere*, 1923. Aquatint and drypoint over heliogravure. The Museum of Modern Art, New York.

37 Rouault at eighty-five, two years before his death in 1958. He is dressed in the surgeon's uniform he wore for painting. On the easel, a late landscape with figures. On the table, his palette, turpentine, brushes, and some twisted, torn paint tubes. He said, "I assassinate them."

DERAIN

To understand French landscape one must visit the Ile-de-France, that region northwest of Paris where small villages nestle in gently rolling hills covered with fruit trees and flowers. The human scale of the land, the humbleness of the steeple of every village church evoke another age.

The highway cuts through the peaceful summer landscape, and I arrived in the village of Chambourcy. In one of the narrow cobbled streets was Derain's house. The high walls that surrounded it were typical of the French hope of privacy. But this is not the poor suburb of Utrillo's Vésinet. This is a nobler countryside, and Derain seemed like the lord of the village. Violent barking answered my ring at the metal gate. A vicious dog ran toward me; visitors were not at all encouraged.

In the small tree-shaded courtyard was the classic façade of a traditional French *petit château*. The doors and windows were high, and the horizontal rows of small square windowpanes rose like small multiple ladders. In this old-world atmosphere my eye was attracted to a discordant object—the chrome and black intricacies of a modern racing car. The contrast of the quiet, sleepy village, the old stones of the house, the badly paved yard with its chickens and barking dogs, and this twentieth-century automotive monster was a key to Derain.

He came out to greet me, tall and massive. His face had the impassivity of a Roman emperor's bust. His weight and frame prevented undignified movement. There was something majestic in his bearing. There was a slowness and sureness about him, and with it a great humanity. Also a certain shyness seemed a protective barrier between him and the outside world.

On the ground floor there was a large studio, probably the old living room of the house. Here Derain kept his printing presses and piles of books and references, and here he worked on his etchings and lithographs. This was really a storeroom. The tiled floor of the large covered veranda was strewn with drying fruit, rose petals, and canvases by Derain.

The veranda with its tall rusty shutters opened on the garden. This unfurnished terrace was also used as a storage for canvases. The unkempt lawn grew high with weeds and grass. The tall man who was showing me around seemed lonely amid surroundings that spoke of past glory. As in many other painters' homes, there were no ornaments in the living part of the house, just the bare necessities, and sometimes even these were absent. There was no need to keep up face, or to live a conventional life with each room having its appointed purpose. That was not the important thing in Derain's life; his work and his mood came first.

He wanted to take me down to his other studio, built down a slope at the end of the garden. Although the distance was only about three hundred yards, we got into a tiny car which seemed like a toy in the hands of this gigantic child. We drove down to the little studio—a modern one, neatly and practically built. Here, surrounded by tall trees, far from the conventional house, Derain was in his element. It was mostly filled with sculptures—cut-out pieces of metal—with hieratic, religious, or pagan themes.

Derain wore a worker's cap. As he sat by his worktable with the knives, pincers, chisels, and hammers, the metal, brass, and copper forms, he looked like a mechanic. He himself was the link between the cap, the tools, the metal, and the Bugatti. When I asked to photograph him, Derain became self-conscious. He kept asking advice: "Should I put on a blue jacket or gray? Which one will make me look thinner?" At first I felt a distance and a difficulty of communication, but gradually I found him one of the most charming human beings I have ever been

67

in contact with. There were simplicity, ease, and naturalness, as well as an intense and subtle dignity in his bearing.

For a moment Derain sat down and placed his hand against his chest. The massiveness of his head, the thick, strong hands, the slow, curving volume of his body gave monumentality to the living Derain. There was grandiloquence in his manner. He reminded me of the great actors of the Comédie-Française. He had a true feeling for theatricality and drama. Seated and posed for a camera, he had a plastic understanding of what a pose should be. I expected him to recite in measured Alexandrines, that chant polished by the French tradition, some ode to nature.

Giacometti had often told me how highly all artists regarded Derain; how they respected his intelligence, and how he was always in the front of aesthetic research. When we dined one evening I was surprised to hear Derain say, "Art must not be intelligent; art is a *jouissance,* an enjoyment."

As I looked at Derain sitting next to his early *fauve* portrait, I thought of his sad life; there was a certain bitterness in his smile and expression. His had not been the easy path to art. He had been one of the wildest of the *fauves;* he had also journeyed with Picasso to the threshold of cubism. His early paintings were highly prized; but he had willfully turned away and struggled to re-create a classical tradition against all the egotism and expressionism that was flourishing among his fellow artists. This single-handed reaction was difficult. Derain, like a dictator, felt that he had the power and strength to lead the way; but the currents against which he fought have flourished and have attracted more and more followers. Derain, instead of gathering masses of young artists to his banner, found himself alone, more or less forgotten and, sometimes, even derided. There have been few Derain exhibitions. Indeed there have been few Derain books. This giant of art sat alone broodingly, stubbornly believing that he was right and all others wrong.

We returned to the house and then went upstairs to another studio. This must have been the old master bedroom with its fireplace, low ceiling, and doors that opened on a balcony. In this seemingly everyday room there was an incredible clutter—paintings, sculptures by Derain, sculptures from other countries and ages, Negro masks, medieval figures, Romanesque sculpture, playing cards, a fabulous accumulation of inspirational objects so intimately mixed that one could not distinguish between them and Derain's own creations. There were humorous portraits of children, prankish heads of men and women, funny caricatures, and by a window with a very strong cross light a still life was in progress. Like Braque, Derain drew in chalk over his oil paint.

All the while, I sensed a mind beating at the artist. As a *fauve* he had been one of the most powerful and dynamic painters of our day. Then, lashed by his discipline, he forced his talents and obediently painted in a classical, seemingly impersonal manner. If the ego was hateful, here was a demonstration of how to tame it. There was intense grandeur in this conflict, in these paintings, and in this man. But Derain felt that the art which was universal and had for centuries survived the passing fancies had some eternal laws. He works under the classical belief that the ugly is the human and the beautiful is both the eternal and the universal.

André Derain. 1880–1954. Born, France.
Photographs taken in 1952.

38 Woodcut from *L'Enchanteur Pourrissant*, by Guillaume Apollinaire, 1898–1909.

39 André Derain in 1952. This large studio is in the garden of his Chambourcy house. He worked in the fields of sculpture, painting, and drawing, practically at the same time. His inventive mind needed to give shape to matter, and rediscover the traditions of past craftsmanship.

40 *Big Ben*, 1904. Oil, $31\frac{1}{8}'' \times 38\frac{1}{2}''$. Collection Pierre Lévy, Troyes.

41 The incredible clutter over the mantelpiece of his small studio in the house itself. On the left, a portrait of Vlaminck.

42 Some of Derain's experiments with sculpture. He was always searching to give expression, permanency, and a new finish. On his property are several baking ovens for his sculpture.

43 Derain at seventy-two, a hard-living, haughty man of the world, with a 1901 self-portrait painted fifty years before, during his *fauve* period.

VLAMINCK

When I met him he wore the tweed jacket, the yellow shirt, the porkpie hat that seem the attributes of a city landowner visiting his farms over a week end rather than the truly rural natural elegance of a man who belonged to the countryside around him.

In the enormous mass of aged flesh, the eyes, though small, seemed enormous. The lids were circular skin pouches that shielded and protected his most precious tool, his eyes. As I looked at the eyes, the bigness of the man, the coarseness of his features disintegrated; I became conscious of a tangible emanation from his eyes. Often artists speak of the tactile sense, of touching with the eyes the visible reality. Vlaminck's eyes were an invisible tactile extension that, like antennae, groped and touched the world around him. His blue pupils appeared to cover the whole eyeball with a metallic glint; the steely indifference of the stare enclosed in the scalelike lids had a brontosaurian grandeur. The pushing-away sensation that came from his eyes was in his whole manner; he resented and pushed away the outside world; his first words were gruff, question-resisting answers. In his hostility to communication there was the interplay of wounded sensitivity and self-sufficient pride. He exaggerated his surliness; having willfully withdrawn from civilization, he hated its intrusion and at the same time wanted to be loved despite it.

Born in 1876 in Paris, he was the son of a Flemish father and French mother. Three years later the family moved to Chatou, now a suburb of Paris. His parents were musicians, who paid little attention to their son's education, but they saw that he learned to play the violin. On his school report card his teacher wrote: "Bad pupil, irascible, generous, impetuous."

In 1899, after three years in the army, he returned to Chatou and painting, earning a living by giving music lessons or even playing the violin in a gypsy restaurant orchestra. That same year he met André Derain; that meeting was the turning point of his life. They were both physical giants; both athletes, both painters, and both lived in Chatou, a small town on the river Seine. There they saw the gray bridges, the green islands, and that mysterious fauna of French rivers, the red-topped barges, the small fishing boats, the bathing establishments. Colors were enriched and blended by the watery haze and jarringly rendered more acute by the violent sensation-intensifying cacophony of river sounds.

The same Seine that, at Argenteuil upstream, opened the eyes of impressionists to color became in Chatou the initiator of the inspired young men experimenting with explosive color. Derain, Vlaminck were to be the founders and only members of the "School of Chatou." In 1901, at the first great Van Gogh exhibition, Derain introduced his friend Vlaminck to Henri Matisse. Later Matisse came to see Derain and Vlaminck at work in their rickety riverside Chatou studio.

The discovery of Van Gogh was the great revelation of Vlaminck's life. He said, "I love Van Gogh more than my father." Vlaminck felt a kinship of blood and spirit, but, above all, the violence of Van Gogh's transcription of emotion corresponded to the yet unexpressed pent-up creative energy in Vlaminck. He was given an outlet, a means of relieving an inner pressure. This key that opened the door of his soul was color.

Fauves or "wild beasts" was the mocking name given to the group of artists who, with Matisse, Derain, Vlaminck at their head, exhibited in the Paris Salon of 1905. They believed in the use of bold, violent, unshaded color, often squeezed out directly from the tube onto the canvas. *"Fauves,"* "impressionists," "cubists" were derisive labels, but time and success made the jokes misfire. The "sticks of dynamite," as Derain called the tubes of color, were triumphantly hurled into the face of the hostile world.

In this struggle mutually stimulating friendships were born, the curious spiritual associations of artistic teams pursuing the same goal. The tandems of Vlaminck-Derain, Derain-Matisse, Braque-Picasso were following the patterns of Gauguin-Van Gogh, of Monet-Renoir, of Pissarro-Cézanne.

The search for who is first is alien to the artist. Matisse, Derain, Vlaminck, Braque, Picasso were enthusiastically creating side by side, discovering, giving to each other and eventually to the world, knowing that love of life feeds on generosity. It is all the more pitiful to find the great artists separated by art classifiers, dealers, and collectors. The struggle to establish rights of discovery is a mockery of creative purity, a money-minded belief in some universal patent office of art. Who was the first *fauve?* Vlaminck maintains that Matisse came to watch him and Derain paint their wild canvases in Chatou. Matisse's admirers brandish dates, proofs to the contrary. Who first "discovered" Negro sculpture and art? Vlaminck and his friends maintain that he was first. He saw an idol in a bar, showed it to Derain, who showed it to Picasso, who et cetera, et cetera. Others credit Picasso or Matisse.

The public has been misled into believing that art is an invention, a creation from nothing by a solitary genius working in a vacuum. Art, like life, which it reflects, is a continuity. The discovery of Japan stimulated impressionism. The enormous Easter Island heads, the hieratic art of Africa, existed for centuries but needed the right time and the right place to emerge and exert their power. Like a virus, such things lie dormant in the artistic bloodstream until a sudden change or shock, or weakening of other creative forces that have kept them subdued, permit their emergence into the collective consciousness.

Derain once said of Vlaminck, "Of us all he is the true painter." No one can take away from Vlaminck his greatness. The length of one's life does not always correspond to one's creative span. Some great artists have produced little; some died young; others, like Vlaminck, lived longer than the changing tastes of the world.

It has become fashionable to attribute greatness only to certain periods of an artist's creative evolution. Through these arbitrary decisions whole segments of inspired research are ignored and belittled. There are so few truly great painters, men who have dedicated their lives to the search, that it would seem that the recognition given to their "great" moments would at least warrant a respectful, sympathetic viewing to whatever new avenues they explore. Vlaminck, Derain are branded as *fauves;* only their *fauve* paintings are sought; but their *fauve* period lasted only six or seven years in life spans of over seventy years. In 1908 both abandoned pure color, partly because they had come under the influence of Cézanne. Vlaminck said, "I suffered when I reached the maximum of intensity and was limited by the blue and red of paint manufacturers."

The dark, brooding landscapes that Vlaminck painted in his last thirty years are against the art current of the time. For Vlaminck the mind is the enemy of feeling, and his long life has been a logical pursuit of that "unspoiled eye" of the primitive. The Negro sculptures were a reaffirmation of permanent essentials.

The proofs of his passion for Negro art still hung in his studio-living room, a dark, large room. This accumulation of masks, figures, heads, helmets, weapons, animals, made the house look like a warrior's trophy room. The black, brown, yellow colors of wood, contrasting with the sickly yellow of ivory and the cold north light breaking in thin bluish-gray slivers on the rough-hewn facets, seemed to create a crystal of light around each dark object.

Vlaminck sat down in a dark red leather armchair, his weight pressing hard on the tired springs. I had a momentary image of a man drowning in fatigue, in old age, gasping for a last breath of air.

In answer to a question he held up two books, *Landscapes and People* and *Portraits Before Death.* "I have nothing to say; all you want to know is written here." He was a writer; he had published a dozen books—from romantic novels to vitriolic pamphlets.

He stood up, went toward the corner near the long, low window, and sat down on a high stool by a tall easel completely splattered with paint. "This easel that you see here is forty years old. I had it in Montparnasse." A curved palette hung on the easel, a large opaque area of black submerging the few bright colors.

Reminiscences started flowing; he forgot his forbidding act. His impulsive nature reassured, the process of communication started. Words crowded the mouth of this solitary man. Nothing could stop him now; his hoarse voice coming out of the hunched, resonant frame filled the room with a continuous rasping.

"Toward 1900 I shared a studio with Derain . . . the rent was ten francs a month . . . even so we didn't pay our rent. We used to burn the wooden chairs to keep warm. The portrait that you see here, I painted it in those days to pay the rent . . . ten frances . . . now, it's worth two million." His mind jumped from subject to subject as a word, a sound, pressed an inner button and released memories.

Lautrec: "He had the intelligence of a hunchback." Vlaminck goes to the movies but protests against their portrayal of artists: "Lautrec loved women and he was never embittered by his deformity."

Utrillo: "The film on Utrillo was equally false. They made him look like some idiot from the Renault factory. That isn't Utrillo. He is out of Dostoevski. There is a little of Alyosha in him."

Rouault: "He's a madman, too. His is a mystical folly. I have letters, poems of Rouault . . . completely crazy. For Rouault, Christ was a rebel."

Vuillard: "Don't like him. A Vuillard smells of cats and musty interiors. Bonnard has much in common with Vuillard, but Bonnard is an honest guy. He's a little master, like the little Dutch masters, who paint interiors with women darning socks and naked babies' bottoms. . . . Bonnard's on the level. But he is a *petit bourgeois* who does not rise above his epoch. Like Proust . . . it does not go beyond his epoch. It becomes old-fashioned, like fashion that becomes unfashionable, like skirt lengths.

"A man who surpassed his epoch, and how, Van Gogh!

"I don't like artists, especially painters. I prefer writers. Literature is my 'Violon d'Ingres.'

"I work fast . . . I am not a Braque who makes tapestry. I never retouch a painting . . . it's better to start afresh on a new one; otherwise one gets lost.

"There is too much calculation in modern art. Me, I've never been able to add. I stand for the painting of feeling."

As he leaned a landscape against a chair he said, "Today we see the world through the road. The gasoline pump has replaced the Virgin in its alcove by the road. One day we went one hundred kilometers to Deauville for dinner. Coming back I saw the gasoline pump illuminated by the headlights of my car. It's in that light that I wanted to paint it, in the beams of light from my headlights. I went back three times to see that gasoline pump."

His whole life had been this struggle for the direct transmission of the artist's personal vision to the spectator. In his youth he thought color could do it; in his later years, form; but his final belief was that the surest means is through sentiment. The emotion experienced in common with others is the truest way for the artist to be understood.

In an interview in 1925 he said, "In art, theories are as useful as a doctor's prescription; one must be sick to believe in them."

Maurice de Vlaminck, 1876–1958. Born, France.
Photographs taken in 1954.

44 Maurice de Vlaminck at seventy-eight, a former *fauve,* a solitary and forbidding man. When I first saw him he stood behind this Dutch door at Rueil-la-Gadelière in Normandy, where he had lived for years in retirement from the agitation of city life.

45 A painting of flowers in Vlaminck's late non-*fauve* manner. He had been using this paint-splattered easel for over forty years.

46 Vlaminck in his studio, curiously dark and Flemish, with tiles and rich wood textures. The Negro masks shine darkly.

47 Four figures from the Baule tribe, Africa, in Vlaminck's collection of African sculpture. He was one of the first artists to discover its beauty and its power, and initiated Matisse, Derain, Picasso, and Braque.

DUFY

Raoul Dufy was a master draftsman. His drawing was the bone of his art. Even his use of color was in terms of drawing. His method of direct, uncorrected statement conferred on his work an apparent spontaneity that was the fruit of years of training. He was the most charming of the *fauves,* expressing his inner violence through the staccato of his strokes.

His studio was in Montmartre. Through the high windows he could see children playing in the cobbled street. Dufy always put on his glasses to paint, and his rounded features took on the pained expression of an old child concentrating. He was seventy-five when I last saw him, and he still worked swiftly, with a few sure strokes, but there were long pauses of doubt and contemplation. The gay, bright final result of his art hid from the world the pain of a sick man and the torment of his creation.

NOTES ON THE ILLUSTRATIONS

Raoul Dufy, 1877–1953. Born, France.
Photographs taken in 1952.

48 Dufy painting in Paris in 1952.

49 In his studio he kept this model of a sailboat, a souvenir of his childhood spent in the great seaport of Le Havre. On the easel, one of his regatta paintings. The scintillation of sails and flags against the blues of sea and sky was a favorite theme of this great colorist. And ever present is the classical sculpture, a reminder of the permanent beauty of feminine form.

VAN DONGEN

One of the first great *fauves,* Kees van Dongen, found in the violence of color the means of expressing his vitality. As a youth he was so strong that he worked as a porter in the Paris Halles. Later in life he has known the debilitating and dangerous success of a painter of celebrities. The who's who of Paris between the World Wars were his models.

His Paris studio with its sculptured decor is of another era. It is so large, so sad and lavish that it made me think of a ballroom on some giant transatlantic liner as it sailed on its last crossing. Imaginary portraits of first-class patrons were its passengers. Kees van Dongen, his beret at a rakish angle, his white beard jauntily trimmed, was in command on the imaginary deck of the studio floor. He seemed a Dutch sea captain, experienced, powerful, the last master of a luxury cruise.

NOTES ON THE ILLUSTRATION

Kees van Dongen, 1877–1968. Born, Netherlands.
Photograph taken in 1959.

50 Van Dongen surrounds himself with art objects from many cultures. I noticed several Egyptian sculptures, a Buddha, Chinese vases. His easel and palettes are set up in the center. Several mirrors about the studio allow him to see his models from a great distance.

MATISSE 22

23 MATISSE

25

MATISSE

26

MATISSE 27

MATISSE 28

A B

C D

E F

G　H

I　J

K　L

30

MATISSE

31

ROUAULT

ROUAULT 33

ROUAULT

38

DERAIN

39

DERAIN 40

41

42

43

DERAIN

45

VLAMINCK

VLAMINCK 46

47

49

VAN DONGEN 50

III
MASTERS OF CUBISM
AND ABSTRACT ART

PICASSO

I am going up to Montmartre," Picasso said after luncheon in Golfe-Juan. He meant, of course, up to Vallauris, where he lived from 1945 to 1955, but the slip or willful change of name revealed the inner link with his heroic, creative youth in Paris and the vital importance that Vallauris, the quiet little hill town on the French Riviera, has played in his life.

On the Mediterranean coast he is close to his Spain. He can attend bullfights in Nîmes, and his Spanish friends can easily visit him. The rocky coastline, the olive oil in the food, the silver light reflected from the shimmering leaves of the olive trees, the intense shadows on the cubelike houses, are necessary to his creative life. In the South he finds that intense contrast of light on dry landscape which has caused almost all Spanish artists' preoccupation with the extremes of light and shadow, forcing them to attain the maximum expression in black and white. In this violent visual contrast is the secret of the Spanish genius for drawing and painting. It is as though the clear, dry southern air forces a clear, precise vision, even of death. The conflict of light and shadow, of black and white, is the conflict of life and death. Spanish art from the sadistic dismemberings of Goya's *Disasters of War* to the iridescent putrefaction of El Greco's *Burial of Count de Orgaz* to the agonizing last gasps of Picasso's *Guernica* has sought to make the idea of death a pictorial reality. In *Disasters of War* and in *Guernica* only black and white could express the artists' indignation at man's inhumanity and death.

The Vallauris villa, high in the hills, is a yellow two-storied house that could have been the house of a local doctor or notary. During the summer, hydrangeas help to give the semblance of a well-kept garden. One day when Albert Skira, the Swiss art publisher, and I went there, we walked around the house with its shuttered windows to the back entrance and the kitchen. Two women were busily cleaning. On the shelves, mixed with cooking utensils and ordinary kitchen dishes, were a few Picasso plates. On the Moresque tiles of the studio-living-room floor stood many paintings; on the walls, souvenirs of bullfights, photographs. A large bookshelf was loaded with objects—books, gifts, mementos, sketches, and photographs, a storehouse of visual impressions, the same unbelievable clutter that is in Picasso's Paris studio.

One of the women told us to go on into the bedroom where Picasso was resting. In the semidarkness of that shuttered room he reminded me of a figure from

his own classical period, a virile god of mythology, his torso covered with gr
white hair. His dark round eyes are so intense that you do not see anything else
his face except the two black piercing dots that hypnotize and hold you. The pe
tration of his eyes is prodigious. His body, old but strongly muscled, is the bo
of prehistoric man. His neck is short and bull-like, his skull deep and large. I
head seems large in relation to the rest of his body. In his seventies he still conve
an impact of primitive strength. He seems incessantly hunting to fix his visu
prey, as the cave artist fixed his prey on the walls of Altamira. His eyes are co
stantly searching form, dimension, movement. All of his gestures are precise a
incisive. A pencil in his hand becomes a scalpel ready to cut the space before hi

In the middle of the small white room stood a big brass double bed ar
near it, a heavily pearl-encrusted Spanish chest, the only piece of luxurious furi
ture. A three-paneled modern dressing mirror covered one whole wall. Over t
top frame of that immense mirror were *banderillas* of red, green, yellow, blue. T
ceiling held a bare bulb. Above the fireplace hung two heads by the Douani
Rousseau, along with portraits by Picasso of his children, and an enlarged pho
graph of Picasso's head, plus a small half-hidden photograph of Françoise, I
wife, from whom he is now separated. The rest of the room was incredibly cl
tered with newspapers, magazines, and letters, all piled high, unopened, waiti
to be thrown out. Picasso, who always wants to answer letters, puts them aside
answer in the evening, then comes home tired, says, "I'm too exhausted, there a
too many of them," and throws them into the wastepaper basket.

When Picasso saw us, he said, "Oh, today is a bad day to see me." He w
expecting some Spanish visitors. He decided to get up and dress—in a polka-dotte
blue shirt and wide, baggy shorts. With his extremely large head, this short, stoc
man seemed like a young boy dressed in his father's clothes. There was a feeli
of youth and at the same time of age; his hair very white, his face wrinkled, a
his voice curiously soft and unsure as he asked questions and listened to the
answers. But his dark eyes wandered. It was hard to understand in those eyes I
changes of mood. One had to rely on his voice and on the extreme mobility
the wrinkles around his mouth. I was struck by his voice. He seemed to speak wi
such uncertainty, the thick Spanish accent coloring his French. Obviously a fe
eigner in France, where he has lived since 1904, he lapsed into Spanish with I
servants, with his Spanish friends, with his son and daughter-in-law.

Everyone milled around. There were the two expected guests, who had a
rived while Picasso dressed. They were from Nîmes, both Spaniards, one a pic
dor, the other a bullfight promoter. (Picasso wanted to organize a bullfight
Vallauris.) They brought with them gaudy, wonderful Spanish bullfight poste
for his selection. While talking to them about the coming *corrida,* Picasso becan
a Spanish peasant. We were joined by Madame Manolo, the wife of the Spani
sculptor. She has been a friend of Picasso's ever since his boyhood days in Bar
lona. To him she seemed like a living letter from the past. There was also Paol
Picasso's son by his first marriage. Paolo, until a few years ago, ran the househo
and acted as manager, chauffeur, and guard. With reddish hair, freckles, ar
heavy muscles, he is like a young, healthy animal. When he smiled he expose
several gold teeth.

The whole crowd walked from room to room, talked of bullfighting, of me

ries of Barcelona; and Paolo, of the various domestic arrangements. Meanwhile
ne great man walked from one to the other, always with an expression of childish
amazement and wonder. He seemed to be surprised at everything—delighted, pleas-
nt, and anxious to put his guests at ease. Time seemed to be of no importance.
eople talked and sat around; there was no urgency about anything, no tension at
ll. Where would one eat? Well, time would tell. For the meantime there was
onversation—not vital talk, just a sort of chatting, as though a group of peasants
ad met on a Sunday in a village square. Later, when we were ready to go out to
at, Skira put on a Tyrolean green hat. It amused Picasso so much that Skira gave
to him. He immediately put it on and looked at himself in the mirror de-
ghtedly. He has a need, a sort of childish desire, to take and to get inside other
eople's possessions. He likes to take, but he also likes to give and see people give.
Ie put the hat on and never took it off until we got to the restaurant. This had
lade his day. The new toy had made possible a new transformation of himself.

A big table was set up at Tétou, a restaurant on the beach of Golfe-Juan.
verybody ordered bouillabaisse and lobsters. Tourists at other tables respect-
ally watched every move. One would get up from time to time and ask Picasso
or an autograph; he was aware that he was watched and his concentration seemed
ore willful than in the relaxed atmosphere of his own villa. He ended his
incheon with vanilla ice cream and chocolate sauce. Paolo particularly amused
im. Picasso likes clowns. He wanted to laugh. I felt as though he forced himself
) laugh louder and stronger than others because deep in him he was extremely
d.

Around three-thirty he decided that he would take me to his studio, back in
'allauris. We drove up to a high wall with a gray weatherbeaten door covered
ith torn posters. Picasso took a large key from his pocket, opened the door, and
e were inside an abandoned perfume factory. Several connecting buildings with
ig double hangar doors are Picasso's creative factory. It seems natural that this
lan, one of the most productive artists in the history of art, has to have a factory
or his creative enterprise. In a corner building he opened a glass door. The first
udio we entered was small and long, like a strange, narrow passage. At one end,
ext to the glass door, stood an easel surrounded with canvases. There is a haunt-
ig resemblance between his Paris and Vallauris studios: they are both vast and
ark.

Picasso works with very little of the painter's essential—light. The little there
comes through the window nearest his easel in a single, intense shaft of sun-
ght, its blinding brightness making everything around it darker. Sabartés,
icasso's lifelong friend and secretary, once said to me, "He does not need light.
. . He has his own light from within."

The long tables were covered with cans of paint; shelves holding boxes of
aint tubes, toy sculptures, his own sculptures; again, insistently present, an
nlarged photograph of Picasso's head. On one table, mixed with the works of
rt, were thirty or forty blue boxes of Gitane cigarettes. He smokes incessantly.

Art is not a spontaneous creation; it needs either art or nature to thrive on.
icasso is surrounded by an unbelievable mass of visual stimulants. All the ob-
cts that have primed the pump of his creativeness are religiously preserved. For
iis man is a collector; he collects everything, everything that pleases, interests, or

111

inspires him. "I never move anything in a studio. I always leave everything exactl
as it is," he said.

Picasso, perhaps fearing that he will lose a source of inspiration, never allow
anything to be thrown away. His houses, his studios show the accumulation of h
long life. Picasso needs all the memorabilia, all the art and sculpture of th
world to inspire him, but to produce he needs little. All has to be reduced t
essentials as uncluttered as the inspirational sources were cluttered. His tools are
few brushes, a few squeezed tubes, some paint pots, a bottle or two of turpentir
and oil, small tablets for palettes. "I use very little oil—mostly turpentine. I mak
my own small palettes out of plywood. I use boat paint—any kind they give me.
This is all Picasso needs in order to create. The rest is in his mind.

The paintings on the easels were very different: one, a sad image of his chi
dren, as if their absence—they were in Paris with their mother—had drained h
eye and mind of all joy. There were other paintings of his children, writing an
drawing, starkly simplified in contrast to the realistic sweetness of his early po
traits of children. In this period, with its opposite accents of green and mauve, c
black and white, red and mauve, there is a sadness, like a deep minor key in
Mozart opera, the end of a chant. There are both a realization of age and an ii
tense appreciation of youth.

Among these paintings was a carefully realistic canvas of a young girl in th
manner of Cranach. On several other canvases there were stylizations and varii
tions on the original head. On the main easel, the final image of the girl, with he
hair in a pony tail, stood as material evidence of the immense filtering proce
leading to his artistic production.

He led me to a drawer and opened it. Inside were about forty pencil drawing
of this girl, all heads, all drawn closer to his early Ingres period than anythin
he had done since. This then was the secret of his method—a completely pene
trating, obsessive, realistic analysis of a thing seen. Only when it was at last full
known and possessed was he free to begin his experiments, slowly, progressivel
destroying the original form to arrive at the minimum of recognizable realit
still sufficient to invoke in him the lingering image. After the first black an
white realistic painting, he had painted twenty or thirty more canvases, each on
abstracting a step further the original portrait; each one reducing to essential
creating a new sign language that would still bring to the mind the image of th
girl with her hair in a pony tail.

"You see this one," Picasso said, pointing to a study of another dark-haire
girl. "I made three of her. In the third one I dominated her, and it is the best; i
the others she dominated me." Somberly he added, "Women devour you!"

"I have a horror of people who speak about the beautiful. What is the beaut
ful? One must speak of problems in painting!

"Paintings are but research and experiment. I never do a painting as a wor
of art. All of them are researches. I search constantly and there is a logical se
quence in all this research. That is why I number them. It's an experiment i
time. I number them and date them. Maybe one day someone will be grateful,
he added laughingly.

"Rhythm is a perception of time. The repetition of the pattern of this wicke
chair is a rhythm. The fatigue of one's hand as one draws is a perception of tim

112

"A painting doesn't exist—it cannot be a simple material object. A painting is a machine to print on the memory. A collector who buys it doesn't buy an object. He buys an intangible, and one day he wakes up with only a frame surrounding a space.

"For me each painting is a study. I say to myself, I am going one day to finish it, make a finished thing out of it. But as soon as I start to finish it, it becomes another painting, and I think I am going to redo it. Well, it is always something else in the end. If I retouch, I make a new painting."

Looking at one of his paintings, he said, "Accidents, try to change them—it's impossible. The accidental reveals man."

Just as his drawings in the drawer were all in black pencil, the original realistic painting was not in color, and the majority of the successive studies were in black and white. To Picasso, form and line are all-important. He even said, "Color weakens." He sees fundamentally in black and white; he is not a colorist in the conventional sense but has the extra vision of a sculptor-draftsman. His great periods are predominantly monochromatic—the blue, the rose, the gray-brown of analytical cubism. Wherever he uses color, it is used to separate form and differentiate line. When I saw him, he was working with two colors at a time. On a small panel of raw plywood were pressed a dab of green, a dab of violet, and that was all; on a similar small panel, a large blob of white, a large blob of black, and that was all. These opposite extremes of color were the only ones in use, an economy of means to achieve the greatest possible contrast and richness.

"One must be able to cable a painting," he said.

Then after a moment's hesitation, he went on, "One can't cable a Rembrandt, but the archaics, the primitives, one can cable their art.

"Painting is really a way of life. I have a need to put things down on canvas or paper.

"I have an extraordinary memory. I remember practically all my paintings. The blue period was not a question of light or color. It was an inner necessity to paint like that."

"Cubism?" I asked.

"I saw that everything had been done. One had to break, to make one's revolution and start at zero. I made myself go toward the new movement. The problem is how to pass, to go around the object and give a plastic expression to the result. The secret of many of my deformations—which many people do not understand—is that there is an interaction, an inter-effect, between the lines in a painting; one line attracts the other and at the point of maximum attraction the lines curve in toward the attracting point and form is altered.

"This change through attraction, that's what the collector never sees and will never understand in a painting," he said contemptuously. "And often one does a painting really for a corner of the canvas that no one looks at. One does a whole painting for one peach, and people think just the opposite—that that particular peach is but a detail."

He looked around him and said, "All this is my struggle to break with the two-dimensional aspect."

To break with the two-dimensional is not only an aesthetic problem. It corresponds to man's need to express a deeper dimension of his soul. Many great artists have revolted against their fate, against the restraints of society, or their inner compulsions. This breaking away is an affirmation of the artist's power. The revolt is a process of contradiction, the artist's choice between two opposites. If he feels the need to destroy that which he has just loved, this is compounded proof of the strength of his attraction.

The grotesque faces, the masks, the tortured monsters of Picasso, like those of Bosch and Goya, are not fantastic visions of another race but images of the artist's compassion and love of mankind. The ugly, the disgraced can be made beautiful by the artist, transformed as if by aesthetic magic. I thought, whatever monsters Picasso conjures up are not frightening, for they are but parodies of a thing loved. Parody, satire, and caricature are often devices to disguise excessive love, extremes to which one leans in order to balance excesses.

Near a tall stove stood some curious shapes of twisted tin, painted gray and then drawn over with black and white. They seemed to be attempts at creating a three-dimensional painting-sculpture. The thinness of the material, the angularity of the drawing, created as dry and pure an effect as that of the great cubist period. This seemed to be a new invention, a new game for this wizard of visual magic to play. He arranged the curious shapes with ease and with knowledge of the power of each interplay.

Picasso, like Michelangelo, seeks to give to painting the three-dimensional power of sculpture. When all Picasso's sculpture can be considered together, he will emerge as one of the greatest sculptors of our time.

In another room, with a higher ceiling than the others, was an immense scaffolding of fresh, raw pine going to the ceiling. This was where he worked on his great murals. In the middle of the workshop stood a weird relic, an enormous black limousine, a Hispano-Suiza, left from the 1920s. Picasso still uses it sometimes. This mechanical monster that he cannot discard is kept as a fetish. He went in and sat down alone in the back, crossed his legs, and for a moment or two was deep in thought, as if remembering the events and places that he had seen in this automobile.

As though locking up a compartment of his creative brain, he locked the studio door and led on tirelessly to another room, where, with another key, he opened the door, this time to an immense room, the largest in the whole factory, a studio crowded with sculpture. A little girl skipping rope was made out of wine baskets. In a corner, a perambulator, made of junk-pile discards, seemed to rock with the weight of a comic-strip baby. This man was playing, trying through play to recapture the innocence of childhood vision, trying through humor to bridge the gulf of years and purge himself of his sophistication. Picasso loves and needs to be near children. He was closest to them there in Vallauris. For his family, through the years a source of freshness and revelation, he has made countless toys, drawn cartoons, played visual games, painted their portraits, each experience enriching him and transferring to him some of the energy of youth.

His agile, playful mind needs such amusement. The sense of humor, the sense of theater, the childish delight in play are underlying qualities in many artists. Maybe one dares more under the excuse of play; the creative act becomes less pompous and self-conscious.

Above the sculpture studio are many small rooms. Over the fireplace of a mall bedroom stood miniature furniture, chairs that would fit in the palm of a hand—his children's toys, and he could play with them too. On a peasant bed lay a book, *A Visit to the Louvre*, and next to the book, Picasso's sketchpad. On it he had drawn from memory, with incredible precision, *Le Déjeuner sur l'Herbe* by Manet and a portrait of Delacroix.

"Painting is a thing of intelligence," Picasso said. "One sees it in Manet. One can see the intelligence in each of Manet's brushstrokes, and the action of intelligence is made visible in the film on Matisse when one watches Matisse draw, hesitate, then begin to express his thought with a sure stroke."

The exactness of the Louvre drawings in Picasso's sketchbook is proof of how accurately his hand re-creates the visions of his mind. He knows art by heart. He knows it, feels it, understands it, and can reproduce it better than anyone living now. He threw himself on the bed and, laughing, flipped through the pages of this re-creation for his children of a trip through the Louvre, or a trip through the history of art.

"To fall back, to live on oneself, to withdraw is sterility. Communication with the exterior means fertility," he said.

"Success is dangerous. One begins to copy oneself, and to copy oneself is more dangerous than to copy others. It leads to sterility." Then, with a smile, he added, "To make oneself hated is more difficult than to make oneself loved."

An artist, as Malraux said of Goya, "discovers his genius the day he dares not to please." Picasso's break with his pleasing blue and pink periods, his caprice to reject successful periods too well mastered and to gamble for the domination of the yet unpossessed are the origin of his inventive greatness.

There are many great painters in the history of art, but few geniuses, few who, having mastered the material problems and techniques in a chosen medium, can transcend the limitations of the craft and from this dominance see beyond ordinary human vision. Picasso can. He is a modern Prometheus, a foreseer, a Titan of the arts. Like Prometheus chained to the mountain where each day a vulture came to tear out his liver, which each night grew again, Picasso is chained to his own greatness and each day his substance is torn out of him in the creative act. This is the ceaseless penalty of men of genius.

Picasso has seen the unseen and of his exploits into the darkness he has brought back proof. His visions do not evaporate like dreams in contact with light.

No wonder he prefers black and white to color. To him black and white are colors, the colors that shine in the two eternally opposed realms of existence, the realms of light and darkness. In a Picasso the intense black outlines and shadows are not the forms and shadows of objects in our everyday life but the color of things brought from the realm of darkness. The flat plane of the canvas is like the frontier between our world and the other. Forms emerge slowly from a Picasso, so that we begin to see them as objects surfacing from a great depth. When they pierce the flat surface of the picture plane, they are struck by the rays of our sun and take on the blinding white color of our reality. The black and white of Picasso are tangible proof that all has two sides, that the essence of things pertains to the two realms.

He led the way to another large hangarlike hall. In this rough plaster-walled room, with its high beamed ceiling like that of an old stable, were stacked against the walls hundreds of Picasso's paintings—large to small, all subjects, all periods. Here this small, powerful man was storing up his accumulation of creation. Here he could come, look, and charge himself with his own vitality.

There is perhaps something of the curator about Picasso in relation to his own work. Each canvas had its year, month, and day written by Picasso in black paint on the back. Even his drawings, unlike most artists', carry a month, day, year, under his signature. He is a collector collecting and cataloguing his own art, creating his own museum in his lifetime. He is even one of the rare painters who buys and collects the works of his contemporaries. In his Paris studio I remember seeing a large Balthus, a magnificent Matisse—*Still Life with Oranges* —and a Modigliani.

Picasso knew total poverty when, as a young man, he first came to Paris from Spain and starved. The habits of poverty are still present wherever he lives. Perhaps that is why he has bought and collected so much. It is a form of security. This search for security through the hoarding of one's own art may have a deeper reason.

The uprooted artist, living outside his own land, surrounds himself with a world of his own making. Most great artists of the past stayed close to their sources of inspiration. They could understand, explain, and portray them. They all benefited from the absence of easy travel and too-easy communication. Perhaps some nonrepresentational art can be partly explained by the lack of rapport between exiled artists and their new surroundings. The expatriate seeks by a private new vision to replace the lost one.

Picasso pulled out a fourth key. "There's a key for each studio," he said, smiling self-consciously. We went into a dark cavelike cellar, another storehouse. There was no light. We had to strike matches, and he finally opened a little porthole, a narrow beam of light blinding us momentarily. When my eyes became accustomed to the dimness, I saw shelves and shelves of pots, plates, vases, the work that he had been doing in the pottery, here assembled and stored. On the earth floor were baked bricks and curved tiles on which he had painted heads and nudes as beautiful as the early Etruscan and Pompeian masterpieces. The handling of earth itself, the mystery of color transmuted by fire are part of his continuous search for the secrets of timeless mediums.

In Paris he has a special glass vitrine holding his most precious relics. There his own small sculptures stand next to the dried skeleton of a bat, along with prehistoric, Etruscan, African, Eskimo sculptures, fetishes, coins, tokens, primitive idols, china figurines, fragments of bas-reliefs, bits of stone and metal, hammered, eroded, chiseled, chipped. In this miniature anthropological museum Picasso's own sculptures are indistinguishable from the rest of his collection. This small vitrine holds the product of centuries of human effort, like a giant test tube in which man's creative germ can be studied, man's ingenuity comprehended. And among these objects his own works find their place in the creative stream of humanity; they seem ageless and universal. He seems superstitiously afraid to touch these things, to disturb them, for fear that his work might be affected. They are the fetishes of his creative life.

Here is no desire to break with the past. Although Picasso is the inventor of new visions, his break is only with the immediate artistic tastes, with the acepted academic schools of his own youth. In a deeper sense, he is a conservative and a traditionalist.

His is not a mind that reasons calmly. Picasso is a violent Spaniard, impetuously striving through his various mediums, painting, sculpture, drawing, lithography, etching, pottery, even writing, to ensnare the heretofore unseen images that will hold his generation hypnotized.

This man lives like a being possessed, a being obsessed with his mission. For a man with Picasso's compulsion a failure to continue to create is death, the living death that comes from self-despising. As Spain's Don Juan needed the constant reassurance of success through repeated possessions in order to preserve his own image, Picasso, to survive, to vanquish his inner fears, has to possess all creativeness. He dares to take creative adventure after creative adventure. His victory over death is his survival through repeated proofs of his own power.

There is anguish in the search which has led him to so many periods of style. He seems to have gone through life with haste, as though his span of life, though long, has seemed too short to him. He has plucked greedily right and left, hoping, by surrounding himself with art, to hold captive and prolong his own creative energy. And maybe in his comparison of so many civilizations, so many modes of art, an eternal law has been made clear to him.

Picasso's art through the decades has seldom shown a constancy of style; his is a contradictory process of attack, then withdrawal, then attack again, each time advancing further than before on the path of artistic discovery. Some natures need a serene, reassuring tempo to create in; others need the stimulus of opposites.

Picasso's inner structure is based on a continuous conflict of opposites. For certain hypersensitive artistic natures, contradiction is an overcompensation for emotional excess. It is a built-in stabilizing mechanism that, like a gyroscope, keeps an excessive nature on an even keel. Contradiction, like an alternating inner current, an oscillation of the mind between contrary and ever-present extremes, is the self-charging source of his creative energy.

Concerned with the unknown and the awesome, his art is seldom a purely joyful statement. But between his distorted, dark periods have appeared, like a recurrent leitmotiv, periods of infinite seduction, of playful, naïve charm.

As if to conform to his pattern of contrasts, in 1955 he left Vallauris and his dark studio to live in a gay sunlit villa called La Californie in Cannes. There the somber key of his late Vallauris period gave way to a sun-wrapped burst of color. In this luminosity he has executed infinite variations on Delacroix's *Femmes d'Alger*. Recently, in addition to the villa La Californie, he has purchased, near Aix-en-Provence, the Château de Vauvenargues, situated near Cézanne's Mont Sainte-Victoire.

Picasso's revolt is always against himself. He destroys the image of a face loved in order to free himself from the servitude imposed by love. He refuses to be the slave of his own admirations. He tries through a progressive stripping off to find the core of the thing loved, to reach his emotional freedom through exhaustive knowledge. Picasso's search for freedom, his craving for a classical detachment, is the hidden backbone of his art. But his attempt at disaffection is doomed, for the more he destroys, dissects, the deeper the final image will be stamped in him and in us. By making this striving visible, he has revealed the profound humanity of artistic pursuit. For Picasso, art is no longer a stern, im personal set of canons, it is a revelation of the fallible in man. Art is a unifying leveling force which brings all together in an understanding, compassionate vi sion. The artist's eye reveals a feeling heart, and through this chink in the aesthetic armor we are made part of the aesthetic experience. We are riveted as we stand before a Picasso by this visualization of an emotional tearing away. The remaining traces of reality in the "finished" canvas give us the measure of the distance that he has covered.

"I have a horror of something finished," he said. "Death is final. A revolver shot finishes off. The not completely achieved is life."

Yet Picasso in his creative life dares to risk death and takes chances as con stantly as the matador does in the arena. Hemingway's great book, *Death in the Afternoon,* is a great help to the understanding of artistic creation, bullfights Spain, art, and Picasso. In it Hemingway points out the importance of the Span ish word *suerte,* which, according to the dictionary, means: chance, hazard, lots fortune, luck, good luck, haphazard, state, condition, fate, doom, destiny, kind sort, species, manner, mode, way, skillful maneuver, trick, feat, juggle, and piece of ground separated by a landmark. In the technical language of the *corrida suerte* means either luck or any move which has rules for the manner of its exe cution. Picasso's paintings, drawings, and sculptures are his *suertes* of art. Each canvas is an arena in which he engages in aesthetic combat. Just as the bullfight has its inexorable laws, an individual work of art has its laws; the artist must perform within the framework.

He has the ability to see and appreciate the unexpected, as the matator must when it appears before his hands and eyes. This ability to choose presupposes an experienced eye and mind. Here Picasso's knowledge of practically all that has been created through centuries of art is in immediate control. To select from the hundreds of thousands of lines that he has traced through his pictorial quest, he must compare, judge, and retain only what goes beyond a previously seen pattern

Picasso's prodigious memory of art serves him well; he is like a giant electronic computer into which the art data of the world has been fed; there it lies stored up until he calls upon it to sort out and eliminate visual duplications and produce an inspired result, all with unbelievable speed.

In the speed and abundance of his work Picasso is truly the artist of the twentieth century. He has understood its tempo and much more. From the rapid frame-succession of the cinema and animated cartoon, he has learned the need of visual surprises, changes of pace, close-ups. He has made his entire creative process into a continuous film sequence; the dating and numbering of his works are permanent indications to posterity of the logical order of succession. His method of mass-production, coupled with an incredible plastic inventiveness, admirably fits the definition of the beautiful as "that which gives the greatest number of ideas in the shortest space of time." This definition by the eighteenth-century philosopher Hemsterhuis has become the basis of advanced contemporary aes thetic research.

Picasso is never unclear; there is never any hesitancy in his art, just as in a bet there is no maybe, the decision must be final. His line is a definite opinion; the line he draws is his signature on the contract with chance.

There is no way out once the contract is made. Each decision and choice be-ween colors or between lines is an intuitive selection based on an inspired belief hat the gift of the artist is to choose correctly. One mistake, one wrong decision, ind the structure is imperiled, the work of art collapses. The ability to win often, o triumph over apparent reason, to have faith in one's instinct, is a measure of n artist's genius.

Like most gamblers, Picasso is superstitious. He knows that his faith in the ccidental, in the so-called laws of chance, is his best guarantee of continued reativity. A gambler, in spite of his faith, is unsure and needs to be confirmed, ncouraged in all he does. That is why much more is involved in a gamble than he apparent stakes. All gamblers play for hidden and much higher stakes. They play for their very existence. Each decision, each toss of the coin, is heads or tails, ight or darkness, life or death. This process of dying, then living is, like the reative process, a constant and vicarious rebirth, a reaffirmation to those who are aught in uncertainty.

There is no end in sight for Picasso; he must never finish gambling, he must never stop creating, for to finish would be an admission of defeat, a submission to leath.

Picasso looked around the large cluttered studio and said sadly, "I am all alone. I do everything myself. No, no one helps me. I am all alone. It's too much or me!"

The enlarged photographs of Picasso's face that look down on his bed and on his easel are symbols of a self-examining personality. The large, noble, im-perial head of Picasso, like a super-Picasso, watches over the small, aged man truggling in the creative immensity of his life. Like a stern image of his con-cience, Picasso watches over Picasso, and Picasso has to account to Picasso. Few an stand the constant gaze of themselves upon themselves.

NOTES ON THE ILLUSTRATIONS

Pablo Picasso. 1881–. Born, Spain.
Photographs taken in 1949, 1953, 1954.

51 *Ambroise Vollard,* 1909–1910. Oil, $36\frac{3}{16}'' \times 25\frac{9}{16}''$. The Hermitage, Lenin-grad.

52 Picasso, master in any medium and one of the important sculptors of this century, in his Vallauris sculpture studio in 1954.

53 The Vallauris studio before Picasso left it to live in Cannes. It shows the usual marks he put on his environments. On the easel, one of his many vari-ations of his children, Claude and Paloma. Behind Picasso, one of the series of heads of Sylvette, and to the right the ever-present photograph of Picasso watching Picasso.

54 *Black Head,* 1948. Lithograph, $25\frac{5}{16}'' \times 19\frac{9}{16}''$. The Museum of Modern Art, New York.

55 Picasso using his curious palette cut from plain wood, with just enough space for two opposite colors, white and black or violet and green. An invention of his to achieve the strictest economy of means.

56 A view of his great studio in the Rue des Grands-Augustins in Paris. He moved there in 1938.

57 Picasso is a compulsive collector, especially of his own work.
A. Paris: In glass cabinets in his studio, his own sculpture next to works of other ages and a bat's skeleton.
B. Paris: In a bookcase, an unexpected wedding souvenir and, above, two small Picassos among jars, birds, and clay pipes.
C. Paris: On the lower floor of his studio, Picasso sculpture.
D. Paris: Children's toys, a matchbox with pins, and a candlestick used in many still lifes.
E. Paris: In still another glass case, long whittled wood Picasso figures cast in bronze, next to prehistoric sculpture casts.
F. Paris: Two Picasso clay figures next to Benin African mask.
G. Paris: Next to reams of yet unused paper, a photographic enlargement of a Cranach and a marionette.
H. Vallauris: On a bookshelf, the first charcoal studies of Jacqueline Roque who plays a major role in his present life.
I. Vallauris: A moment of past splendor recaptured. His Hispano-Suiza from the twenties is preserved and is now still used on great occasions such as a bullfight.
J. Paris: His entrance hall. Left, a Negro-period Picasso; right, a photograph of Ingres' *La Grande Odalisque;* and, in the center, Picasso sculpture of fantastic flowers cast in bronze.
K. Paris: In the accumulated clutter of bottles, jars, oil lamp, frames, and small Picassos, a photograph of his son Paolo.
L. Paris: In another corner, again an oil lamp and sculpture by Picasso of his friends, and an imprint of a hand.

58 Three of Picasso's four children, Paolo and the two youngest, Claude and Paloma. Maïa, his oldest daughter, is missing. He is proud to have become a father after seventy.

59 *Maïa,* 1938. Oil 28¾″ × 23⅝″.

60 Picasso lying on his bed at Vallauris, explaining to his son Claude what to look for in a painting. Picasso sketched quickly the cast of characters in Manet's *Déjeuner sur l'Herbe.*

PICASSO

PICASSO 57   A   B

C D
E F

G H

I J
K L

BRAQUE 61

III

Continued

MASTERS OF CUBISM AND ABSTRACT ART

BRAQUE

In Normandy, near Dieppe, the Varengeville studio of Georges Braque is an immense room with a high ceiling. It is shut off from the outside world. It is a world
of its own, Braque's world. In the warm and diffused light, I found myself standing in a luminous womb.

Each ray of the sun is softened and controlled. Instead of clear glass in the
windows, opaque and milky panes disperse an extraordinary glow. The traditional
northern light surrenders to the warmth of the sun which penetrates the studio.
The walls and curtains are white; the floor is covered with a straw mat. Everything is preconceived; each space contributes its allotted function to an organized
creative factory. One receives an impression of unaffected cleanliness and order.

Braque divides his studio into separate areas, like the stage of the mystery
dramas in the Middle Ages: areas for engraving, for drawing and water color, for
relaxation, and, the largest, for painting. On several easels, I saw different canvases simultaneously in progress. They looked like parts of the studio, the studio
like parts of the paintings. There was no divorce.

Flat silhouettes, cut out of white paper, hung in various parts of the room,
were repeated in the paintings. On one canvas posed a large bird; on the wall appeared the shape of the same bird cut out in white. In another place I saw the
silhouette of a flower. Indeed, wherever I looked there were bouquets. Small, as
were all the spots of color in the studio, these bouquets of flowers corresponded to
the small spots of red on his otherwise monochromatic gray palette. It seemed as
if Braque's visual stimulation from color became more intense in relation to the
smallness of the stimulus itself. Any larger bouquets in the room were monochromatic; dried corn, dried thistles. With their intense composition and pointed
design, these arrangements were already still lifes by Braque.

Many sources of visual inspiration decorate Braque's surroundings. In Paris,
he has rubber plants, Polynesian shields, Etruscan sculptures. In the country, on
a wall, hangs a large Indian rug of red and gold. Scattered around are small
stones, pieces of wood, bits of bleached bones. Such carefully selected groups of
outdoor memorabilia as starfish, pebbles, and net create harmonies which Braque
quotes and translates into his paintings. Thus the picture of a bouquet of flowers
and a jug assumes the hues of objects brought in from the beach. On little wire
stands, built by himself, rest several of his bas-reliefs, reminiscent of early
Minoan art. Next to his own sculpture lies the big pink shell of a crab on which

nature has drawn its own design. There is a consonance between the two. Meta-morphosis is the philosophy which underlies Braque's study of natural objects: everything made by God can be selected and transposed by the artist.

Behind his easels hang movable panels of natural sackcloth and fabrics painted brown and gray. Against these somber backdrops, the white accents of his paintings stand out vividly. Braque said, "I want my paintings to be as hard as a flint, so that when struck by eye and light sparks fly."

He is a thinker and philosopher who speaks at random: "Try to see the ob-ject, under many angles, but not through *trompe-l'œil*. One has to try to give a tactile value, first by texture, by the feeling of space." And then, in apparent con-tradiction to his cubist paintings, he repeated, "But always, always avoid *trompe-l'œil*.

"We must go back to the human, not to the man. Today it's the painter who exhibits himself." Braque believes that we must go back to the universal and not stress the accidental individual. His conception is deeply rooted in the classical French tradition, which defines the ego as "hateful."

"One does not say Cézanne is 'talented'; one can say that of Manet. Cézanne's greatness is in his classical impersonality.

"One must take the object and raise it very, very high," he said. "One must have an established dimension because one needs discipline. Bonnard took the other road. Bonnard was a *symphoniste*. He painted on a huge canvas fixed on the wall. He added and added and enriched.

"There are two kinds of painting, hard and soft, with and without the disci-pline of an imposed dimension. Painting is very difficult. The good painting is the solution of all these difficulties and differences of space, tactile value, and color."

During one of my visits, Braque mused about the mystery of why there are certain regions, even in France, where no painting has developed. "Strange how in parts of the world where there is stone you have sculpture, and in the coun-tries of light you have painting."

Intensive preparation goes into his work. In pencil and ink he sketches on thinly squared paper, then makes many preparatory gouaches, sometimes cutting out the principal forms in paper. He creates slowly, putting a work aside, develop-ing another, returning again to what he has started, drawing in white chalk over the oil paint. He works close to the texture of his canvas; then he sits down, relaxes, looks at his work on the easel and, from a distance, at the subjects he is painting. Simple objects, through concentration and silence, assume additional meaning. They are divorced from their ordinary significance. There is an incan-tational quality in his brooding and contemplative appraisal. "The painter," Braque remarked, "must have conscience and loyalty toward his materials and himself to avoid the deterioration of painting."

There is a profound and practical craftsmanship in Braque's work. One feels this in his love of building things himself, of mixing and studying his materials as a housepainter does.

Small details are revealing: the arrangement of his studio, the meticulously studied heights of his worktables. The unique system of louvers, made of light-brown paper, suspended in vertical squares breaks the light over the areas where he is painting. He uses corrugated cardboard to hold pencils and pens—each groove storing many stubs. The stands holding the palettes are made of rough tree trunks, the bark and moss left on, with pieces of iron braced in for support. On different levels of the unique central stem are different palettes, each carrying its own harmony of colors. Braque enjoys making things out of wood and iron. He feels that the act of building something yourself, understanding how two pieces of wood dovetail, is essential to good construction in art. Another practical invention stands between two easels: his sketchbook on a lectern, as in a church, to be used as a visual dictionary of reference and inspiration. Tools are conveniently at hand for every creative need. From his easel he hangs empty tomato cans or discarded cans of any kind. In each he mixes a certain quantity of paint which is the dominant tone of a given area of canvas. In this way, work is not interrupted by the mixing and matching of colors, and a greater continuity is assured. He has an abundance of clean paintbrushes, stuck like bouquets in earthenware jars.

There is nothing in Braque of the mannered *artiste peintre*. There is, however, the modern elegance of a practical mechanic who is not afraid to use any means. He lives in the present and with the creative stream of his time. His studio in Paris was built for him by the great modern architect Auguste Perret; in the country Braque installed, next to a French naïve painting, an armchair by Eames.

Braque is a *grand seigneur* in art. He has raised the material standard of the artist to its highest possible degree. The conception of his studios is grand and noble; they are like the throne rooms of Renaissance princes, but bare and neat and pure. There is no outward show of luxury, but luxury is everywhere: luxury is in the peace of Braque's life, in its spaciousness, quiet, and convenience. Life seems to center around him, and everything is planned to help his work. He has solved the material problems of creation.

At seventy-eight, with his pure white hair, he seems a much younger man. There is great humanity and penetration in his pale brown eyes. He weighs and compares you, the surroundings, your actions, and disappears, withdraws, into meditation. He is quiet and seems to live in a world all his own. But his exterior calm suggests a man who constantly dominates and disciplines his emotions. A sudden smile, a quick movement of his sensitive long hands, however, reveal a hidden warmth and humor.

His country house, separated by some fifty yards from his studio, was built in 1931 in the low and traditional style of a Norman peasant hut. There is a revealing difference between the modern architecture of his "work temple" and the intimacy of his home. The walls of Braque's living room are painted in different shades of warm yellow-orange; the furniture is made of dark wood. Brass and silver platters, spoons and forks, wrought metal of old design hang on the walls. Into this dark house intense light pours from small windows hung with bright yellow curtains; there is the gleam of light on silver, metal, sculpture, and the intense vibration of color from fruits and meticulously arranged bouquets. Flowers again are everywhere, in bold, unexpected arrangements made by his wife. He has been married to Marcelle Lapré for almost fifty years. Together they have lived the exciting struggle of twentieth-century art.

Madame Braque entered, a small, serious woman, with extraordinarily tender, perceptive blue eyes. Under her smart, simple hat the eyes and the nervous curve of her mouth expressed intelligence and wit. She is adored by their friends and amuses them with countless anecdotes. Music plays an important role in her life—her favorites, as well as Braque's, are Bach, Vivaldi, Mozart, and Buxtehude; she owns Erik Satie's piano.

On the lawn in front of the house, a tent had been set up. Some biscuits were brought out, and again the refinement of all Braque's life was revealed. The biscuits had been warmed. We drank his favorite white wine, Muscadet, a fragrant, airy wine, innocent and easy to drink under the midday sun.

He insisted that I visit the church and marine cemetery at Varengeville. The small twelfth-century edifice, built right above the steep cliffs that dominate the northern beaches of France, and the cemetery with its hundred tombs and crosses are in harmony with Braque's colors. The church is gray; the cemetery crosses are of white marble. The stained-glass windows inside, and the black wrought iron and living or artificial flowers outside, contribute vivid accents. The steel-gray expanse of the northern pebbled beach, overcast with the shadows of the high cliffs, creates the dominant black of Braque's marines. I understood how much Braque had absorbed the countryside around him.

The Norman terrain is rich and varied in inspirational substance. There is no flatness and little monotony. The shrubbery, the vales, and the trees that surround his house, the narrow, winding roads with their small cottages, contrast with the deep high cliffs of the beach, the sea color, the fog and haze over distant beaches. The pebbles, the weeds, the shells, the crabs contrast with the cows, the grass, the birds, the fruit trees of this rich Norman country; all are constant stimulation to the mind and eye of a painter.

Here life continues a timeless serenity which our civilization has overlooked. One can still eat pink, freshly caught shrimp in hotels which are reminiscent of Proust's world—where vacationing Parisians dress in blue blazers and white flannels. There is no desire to enjoy quickly, to squeeze hastily the last ounce out of life.

Away from the country, Braque manages to re-create a peaceful existence in the Paris street, the Rue du Douanier, near the park Montsouris. This steep, short dead end with rough cobblestones and small gardens simulates the tranquillity of a small provincial town rather than the capital.

The beige-brown brick façade of Braque's spacious house is ornamented by the black-painted ironwork of the doors and windows, and is in harmony with his predilection for sumptuous browns and blacks. In front of the tall modern windows grow rows of giant sunflowers. Inside the house, the pale gray walls of the entrance hall seem to spiral upward with the sweeping curve of the gray-carpeted stairway. As with everything associated with Braque, the subtlety of the decor, the thickness of the carpets immediately create a feeling of restrained luxury.

As in Varengeville, the living quarters have a Flemish intimacy and richness of texture. On the ground floor, off the entrance, a living room connects with the dining room. Braque's own paintings dominate the two rooms furnished with dark woods and subdued fabrics. Some of the paintings are among his earliest, as if through their presence the master can see at a glance the evolution of a lifetime.

The whole top floor, the studio, like the nave of a cathedral, symbolically crowns the architecture of Braque's everyday life. This studio is the head of his house, the summit to which he has to ascend before he can start to work. Here, as in Varengeville, the light is transformed into Braque's personal illumination by a complicated series of white curtains. I have always felt that this light is softened as if silenced; and, in the hushed luminosity, the contrast between objects ceases as they lose their individuality and fuse into their environment. This knowing manipulation of perception creates a unique universe. Air, space between things acquire tangible substance; all matter seems unified; all things in the room exchange substance—reality becomes purposely deintensified. As a scientist needs to dilute a rich substance to study it better, so Braque reduces jarring reality in order to live with it and study it better. This process of possession, the absorption and digestion of visual phenomena through the use of light, is one by which Braque's rendition of reality acquires mystery. The miracle of plant life is based on the transformation of light into energy; maybe photosynthesis is the image of Braque's creative process. First, slow contemplative assimilation is made possible by the manipulation of light; then inspiration, like chlorophyll in a plant, makes growth and expansion possible. Light is the energy behind the creative restitution that is the act of painting.

Braque was sitting in a corner of the studio on a low couch, surrounded by pillows, protected from the wall by coarse African woven mats. In this niche he could rest and observe his work, with his back to the light, his face in the dark shadows. The pure white of his soft, gently undulating hair shone like an aureole. Since he had been ill, he found that working on a very low chair with a miniature easel no higher than the chair helped his breathing. The vast expanse of floor, unobstructed by furniture, was curiously animated by many small Braque paintings. Seen from the low couch, they created a feeling of receding motion, as if a traveler glimpsed fugitive vistas.

These canvases, mostly views of beaches, were staggered around him like diminutive stage sets. They let his eye wander on the nature he loves and misses when he works in Paris. "When I long for Varengeville, I paint my postcards, these seascapes," he said with a smile. Between the carefully arranged views were old newspapers covering the floor and, on them, pots, rags, brushes, knives, palettes—the paraphernalia of the painter's art. For him, art is not only inspiration hastily transcribed; like a ritual, the actual process of execution gives to the work of art an added meaning.

When Braque in his art reaches a point where all the expected, the known, is magnificently portrayed, he is then able to go further, beyond the security of the tangible, inventing in the process a new sensuality, a sensuality of the spirit. His greatness is in his ability to explore the other reality beyond the one that is visibly lit. The unknown begins when he leaves the protection of light. He is not afraid of night, and the fathomless blacks that recur in his paintings are not shadows; they are his signals warning us of the mystery that lurks behind the surface. They are the visual evidence of the solidity of the artist's pictorial foundation and of his awareness that solid art has to dig deep to find the security hidden in the unknown, the unexplored.

I have had many conversations with Braque, who, for a painter, is particularly articulate about his art. "The painting materializes in contact with nature.

Painting is a meditation. It is contemplation, for the painting is made in the head. One must regurgitate it. One must give it back. Painting is a restitution.

"Light is a delicate thing. There is a confusion made between the effect of light and light itself. Light for a painter has only one purpose—to define clearly his subject, not to make him reproduce some luminous effect.

"Take the preparation of the idea of a picture. If I am going to paint a lobster, all I like to make sure of is whether it has six or four legs. Curious, the visual memory that one has. I did not know exactly how many legs a lobster had, but in drawing it from memory I found the correct number. I discovered that the memory of the appearance rendered the right number. Contact with nature is all the more important because it is constant. An impregnation results to which all artists submit."

I asked if nature exercised a control, a discipline upon him. He answered, "Nature acts on me practically without the slightest control. I have realized that in my whole life I have never had an act of authority. It is strange but it is true."

When I asked Braque if he didn't have to make decisions in painting, he said, "No, my painting is not premeditated. It is a need. I do not see the will appear in it. If that were the case, one might say that an alcoholic is an example of maximum will-power. But that is not will-power. Like the alcoholic who takes his little glass in the morning, I take up my brushes, just like that—without knowing. I am a little drunk. There is no will in that. It is a deep need, like hunger."

"But in your cubist period," I said, "you attempted to make nature fit into a system."

"Yes," he said, "then there was a dominant idea. An idea must be conducted, the will has an action. It was because of this that I did not sign my paintings of that period. They were not, properly speaking, mine. They were my ideas; however, I always wanted something deeper."

Later, speaking about color, Braque said, "It is very complex. For me, color should not be, and is not always, attached to the object. In painting, if you find that an orange is yellow, the yellow can perfectly well be placed elsewhere than on the orange. It was because of color that I made my collages. In them the colors are definitely detached from the objects."

Another time Braque told me, "I do not believe in any one thing. I do not believe in this, or this [he touched an object on a small table]. I do not believe in things; I believe only in their relationship, in their circumstances. Circumstances bestow reality on things. In Zen it is said, 'Reality is not this, it is the fact of being this.' This is a paper knife, but if I use it as a shoehorn, it becomes a shoehorn. For things to exist, there must first come into being a relationship between you and the things, or between the things themselves.

"The poetic for me is to instill things with circumstantial life, to let the circumstances in which they appear serve them. One time, I explained this to a young poet. He said to me, 'I do not quite understand.' I told him, 'You will see. Once I was in my car and the brakes weren't working very well. I stopped on the top of a hill, became frightened, and then began looking around me for something to prevent the car from dashing away. I saw some stones, picked one up, and out of this stone I made a wheel block. That is a poetic transformation, a stone becomes a wheel block. I returned the stone to its place. I went away. It does not exist any more. It becomes whatever someone else will make of it, I do not know what.'

"Everything is based on relationship. The relationship of man and woman brings forth a child. It is the same with the artist and the motif, which together make a painting. But no one looks at the artist or the motif; they are unimportant. It is the painting that results from their relationship that counts.

"It is strange. Take Claude Monet. In the beginning he was very impressionable; his painting resembled much more the mother than the father. When one looks at an early Monet one says, 'How beautiful the atmosphere over the cliffs, et cetera.' For me, that represents the mother. But later, when he started on the cathedrals, one says, 'What a marvelous painter, what an eye!' That is the father revealing himself.

"In a male-female relationship, if there is a mating, it is an image that corresponds to the truth. What is of interest is that which is born from the encounter. Penetration, reception give a result. All nature is that, nothing escapes that. That is what I mean about Claude Monet. The feminine and the impressionable appear in his early work, when the mother is dominant. The mother—that is what I call nature."

"What part does the artist's idea have in a work of art?" I asked Braque.

"I have written," he answered, " 'The painting is finished when the idea has disappeared.' The idea in a painting is like the launching cradle of a ship. It is like the scaffolding used in the building of those enormous ships. After the ship is built, it floats; it has left the cradle useless and forgotten. The idea for a painting is similar. You use the idea to build, to guide, and, when your painting is strong enough, it goes off. It floats; it no longer needs the idea to uphold it. It goes off to lead its own life, as the ship does.

"The image of reality that remains in the finished painting is not the idea. What remains is what comes from the spectator and the painting together, from the relationship between the two. As soon as a spectator looks at a thing, he makes it his own; he brings to it his desires, his needs, turning it into something altogether different. The artist does not retain control of his work in the imagination of the spectator. On the contrary, that's the beauty of it.

"The attempt of the artist should not be to convince people but to make them reflect. I do not ask them to have a definitive opinion, but if a painting of mine can make them reflect, think a little, that is very good. Something of me comes out in my paintings. Well, it is the same for the person who looks at them. The only thing that counts for him is what comes out of himself. It is in that that he must find his life."

We were discussing this when he said, "No intellectuality; one must live in reality. In our epoch, people are preoccupied with science, confused by trying to reduce everything to science. Of course science is something very good, but it does not go beyond intelligence, whereas art only begins when it does go beyond intelligence. Then art touches the soul. Science speaks only to intelligence. One needs more and more art, after all, to rediscover the true reality.

"The philosophers have greatly confused humanity. They have been seeking definitions, but there are no definitions. Happiness, like many things, ceases to exist as soon as you try to lock it up in a definition. Happiness starts where the unknown begins. Happiness is not something promised—it is existence itself."

Braque suddenly asked if I had noticed the portrait of his grandmother in the dining room downstairs. "It is one of my first canvases. I had just finished my military training and I was twenty years old."

There were, even then, traces of Braque's inescapable stamp, I remarked. He said, "Yes, my hair has grown white, but one can recognize me. My painting has grown white, but one knows that it is mine.

"I sometimes have the impression that it is not me who did my paintings. I feel absolutely detached at first glance. It is absolutely as if they were someone else's. But when I concentrate, then I see a lot of things. I recognize my own quirks, the marks of my style. One's style—it is in a way one's inability to do otherwise. The physical is in command. Your physical constitution practically dictates the shape of the brushmarks, as it does the pen marks in writing.

"Especially in the layout of my paintings," he pointed out, "one can recognize master lines that are always in the same place. It is strange—a framing that one makes sensation fit into but that is practically defined beforehand.

"One achieves this by instinct. I have never wanted to bar a way to myself, to be closed up with principles. I accept that which comes truly out of myself.

"Personality is good if it reveals itself without the artist's becoming conscious of it. There must be no exploitation of personality. As soon as a thing becomes conscious it becomes dangerous.

"As soon as an artist becomes aware of his talent, then he is in danger. I have a horror of talent because it is a thing learned and becomes too facile if one ceaselessly refers to it. It is a facility that prevents one from being sensitive to many things. One should go beyond it.

"As a matter of fact, this search for what lies beyond talent stamps our epoch. This tendency is quite contrary to the spirit of the sixteenth and seventeenth centuries. In the Renaissance, painters did only that which they knew how to do. They studied a great deal, but they never did that which they did not know how to do. They did not go beyond the limits of their talent. In our day, though, since Cézanne, talent is not enough. There is here an aspect that could practically be called heroic. To my way of thinking, there is no master to equal Cézanne, who took risks and searched for himself all his life.

"I have always wanted to actually live things instead of representing them. It has been said by a Japanese painter that 'One must penetrate a thing in order to be able to draw it.'

"The Renaissance painters painted what they saw, but I feel that is not enough. One must paint what one feels, at a greater depth. When I am making a sculpture of a horse, when I am working on the leg, I raise mine. The Renaissance masters represented things, they did not live them, in my opinion. That is what gives the theatrical aspect to the Renaissance. The painters confused composition with staging. It was opera and stage directing. But with Cézanne composition is really painting, it is thought out."

When asked if the stamp of our epoch was on his art, Braque said, "I have never tried to trace it. I never try to define precisely. If you try to define a thing, you replace the thing with the idea you have of it, which is generally false. In my art I have said what I have said."

142

However, he is certain that environment subconsciously influences a work of art. "I once told a young painter who spoke to me of his search for originality, 'You are perhaps original, but you are above all a painter of the twentieth century. As soon as you have felt the influence of your epoch you will cease to worry about originality.' Then, too, the small details, the trees, the flowers that surround an artist's life are very important. But it is difficult to define their influence because, contrary to what one may think, environment does not act directly. It is noticeable only when a great deal of time has elapsed. Still, if you put side by side paintings from different countries, you can see the influence of the original surroundings.

"I would like to write on the importance of art in life, on its influences. One cannot begin to imagine the place it occupies, and its effect even on things that seem remote from painting. If nowadays you see so many people on the beaches, going swimming, it's thanks to the impressionists. They were the ones who created the cult of the outdoors. It is so true that if you look at the railway posters encouraging tourism, you'll see that many of them are impressionistic. I could cite many examples like that, a quantity of influences.

"I was very happy when, in 1914, I realized that the Army had used the principles of my cubist paintings for camouflage. 'Cubism and camouflage,' I once said to someone. He answered that it was all a coincidence. 'No, no,' I said, 'it is you who are wrong. Before cubism we had impressionism, and the Army used pale blue uniforms, horizon blue, atmospheric camouflage.' "

With a circular motion of his head, he swept his gaze across his accumulated canvases and said softly, "They populate the studio and they take so much space. I really need another studio." It was moving to hear this old master yearning for more space to fill. "I now paint larger and larger. I would like to add another story to this house."

When Braque stood up amid this multiplicity of objects, his tall figure acquired a new, gigantic stature, contrasted against the Lilliputian reductions of nature that he had compressed into each small canvas. The little paintings were principally studies, but towering above them around the walls of the studio were large finished canvases, his series of birds in flight, no particular bird, but a synthesis of different impressions.

Braque said, "The bird theme started in the thirties, and the sea gulls and the ravens of Varengeville have influenced me very much. So have the birds on the game preserve of the Camargue. There are extraordinary species of birds there, right in the midst of the black bulls. You can see the ibis, the flamingo, and the heron, a magnificent bird. The flight of the heron is beautiful."

The largest canvas of all, like an immense icon, hung in the center of the majestic arrangement of paintings. In this great work of Braque's one gigantic bird hovers over a nest. The bird is gray-white, the background dark brown-black. There are no other colors; the somber, tragic mood is relieved only here and there by unbelievably subtle variations of paint, patina, and texture. My eyes were riveted to this haunting vision.

Braque sat silently watching his work, then said, "It goes beyond painting. Painting is something more than just decoration. There is more to it than composition. There has been too much insistence on aesthetics."

The bird itself, painted in thin layers of whites and grays, seems all the more dematerialized against the rich, sensuous background of lavishly spread paint, as if Braque wanted to emphasize that beyond *matière*, beyond the physical aspect of art, there is an imponderable. To express it he needed the minimum of substance, the minimum of paint in the area of greatest meaning. This economy of expression, this withdrawing of means, is an indication that here in the bird the artist approached the core of his art. It seems as if he feared to touch the surface even with the softest brush. For in this realm where substance is metamorphosed into idea, mystery begins.

"One cannot put this mystery into words," Braque told me. "It is beyond anything one can say. It is the manifestation of an indefinable feeling.

"Art tends toward *le néant*, the state of nothingness, the void. For me, perfection is a sort of nonexistence. It is a realm in which words lose their value. If a thing is perfect, one does not say it is bad or good.

"Harmony is just that state in which one can no longer say anything. It is a joy. Words are valueless, for the word destroys all."

Looking at the bird, I understood what Braque meant when he said, "Happiness starts where we cease to know." He told me, "The bird is the summing up of all my art—it is more than painting." Braque will not sell this *Grand Oiseau*. He will not even part from it for a short time. He said, "When I go to Varengeville, I take it with me."

"It has a hypnotic power," I said.

Braque quickly added, "That's it. It is as if one heard the fluttering of wings."

Plato had conceived of the soul as having wings, "The soul . . . when perfect and fully winged soars upward." About twenty-three hundred years after Plato, Braque, through meditation, achieved the pictorial image of the philosopher's vision. The winged flight in space is the essential preoccupation of Braque's late period.

The bird is the symbol of flight. This symbolism of winged flight as a supernatural condition has been used in poetry and religion, in mythology and legend. Man tied down to earth needs wings to soar into the sky of hope.

There are inner states for which adequate words cannot be found; for a painter-poet like Braque there are moods that cannot be transcribed exactly. All the artist can do is to suggest and, by describing as much as he can of what surrounds that particular hard-to-express mood, make the spectator guess at the hidden meaning. This suggesting and guessing, like the meeting of two intuitions, is the hidden language of art. When art is able to convey the unsaid, the unportrayed, by precisely guiding the spectator's mind into the artist's mystery, it attains its truest grandeur. That the great artist can be understood beyond the merely visible message is proof that he possesses the language of the soul. In our lives we are surrounded by the unsaid, the unheard, the unseen, but only the artist and the mystic can tap this fathomless reservoir. A great work of art will show traces of the exploration of the reality beyond everyday reality. Few are those who know of its existence; fewer still are those who recognize it when it is brought before them through a gift of the artist.

The theme of Braque's series of birds is the theme of solitude. The creative man is aware of his solitude, but his cries in words and sounds are heard by few ears, his image seen by few eyes. He is a prisoner caged in by the everyday reality of those who do not see and hear. But in his dungeon, through a narrow chink of hope, he glimpses a minute area of light, of sky, to which his spirit flies. Alone, he will survive through a ceaseless faith that his cry will be heard, his work understood; that his love of life expressed in his re-creation of it will be loved.

In the brown-black dungeon of Braque's great canvas, the solitary bird flies motionless, carrying its eternal, changeless message, the passage of an inspired cry of desperate love. This cry is the artist's means of communing with the divine, the immortal. The words of Shelley on his art apply to Braque the painter—"Poetry redeems from decay the visitations of the divinity in man."

Where the material world ceases, where the unknown begins, man's faith is born. Faith is the unspoken word, the clue to "beyond painting." Now all seems clear—the white bird in its flight, like the dove of the Holy Ghost, is the symbol of man's purest aspirations, of man's eternal hope of purification through the silent breath of prayer.

NOTES ON THE ILLUSTRATIONS

Georges Braque. 1882–1963. Born, France.
Photographs taken in 1948, 1953, 1956, 1957, 1958.

61 *Houses in L'Estaque,* 1908. Oil, 28¾″ × 23½″. Collection Rupf, Bern.

62 Georges Braque in Paris in 1948, at the age of sixty-six. He likes to wear the French workman's *bleus,* or blue overalls.

63 The display wall of his Varengeville studio. He usually works on several paintings at the same time. On the easel, which belonged to his father, is the bird he calls "the spirit of the studio." This painting is one in his great series of *Ateliers.* On a stand that he made of rough tree branches is his open sketchbook. On the left, the painting *Ajax* and a sculpture. The studio, built in 1948 according to Braque's own logical plan, faces unconventionally south.

64 Braque's Varengeville house, built in 1930, is in the style of the Norman peasant cottages familiar to his childhood. Each wall of the living room is a different color; ocher, yellow, orange. On an antique Norman chest stand one of many bouquets of flowers; a head, *Hesperis,* which Braque chiseled out of stone from the Varengeville cliffs; a pewter teapot that often appears in his lithographs; and an oil and vinegar set he made of two mineral-water bottles. On the wall, Spanish roasting forks.

65 In Varengeville's ocher cliffs, in the beach and sea are grays, blacks, greens, and blues, the color harmonies of Braque revealed in the northern light. There he used to take long walks and rides through the countryside on his motorcycle or in his latest Italian sports car.

66 Braque's profile in front of his *Grand Oiseau.*

67 A. Paris: On his drawing desk, corrugated cardboard holds his pencils, brushes, pens.
B. Paris: Braque's painting utensils. He likes to mix large amounts of color in discarded cans, to be sure he has the identical color for given areas.
C. Paris: In a separate sculpture studio, his sculpture tools meticulously arranged.
D. Paris: He also uses his drawing table for writing his business correspondence.
E. Paris: Braque has the greatest number of paintbrushes of any painter I have seen.
F. Paris: Because of his difficulty in breathing, he has started lately to work on a very low easel, using the floor as a worktable.
G. Varengeville: Madame Braque.
H. Paris: Shadows of leaves on the steps of Braque's garden. He plans the planting himself.
I. Varengeville: Braque surrounds himself with patterns for visual inspiration. A rug, pewter, thistles, wheat, crabs, a paper cutout, all serve the needs of the artist's eye.
J. Paris: The texture and shape of bones inspire him.
K. Varengeville: Braque made this palette stand himself out of a tree trunk and twisted wires.
L. Varengeville: Pebbles, net, a starfish from the beach.

68 Braque's Paris house; the ground-floor living room opens into the dining room. On the left, an early *fauve* landscape, a magnificent analytical cubist Braque, and a Braque sculpture, the bronze head of a horse.

69 Some of the great admirations of Georges Braque. He keeps these special joys behind a door seldom opened to visitors, a door that leads from his big studio to his small sculpture studio. The cofounder of cubism keeps in daily view two black and white enlargements of two Corot portraits, far left; six flower prints; and, below them, a reproduction of a Renoir nude. At the far right, a color reproduction of the Van Gogh *Sunflowers* and a photograph of a detail from the St. John fresco painted in 1353 by Matteo da Viterbo on a wall in the Palace of the Popes at Avignon. The white Fang mask from the Belgian Congo hangs over a beautiful confusion of expected African sculpture, two Braque fish sculptures, bowls and pitchers, a guitar, and, beneath the Van Gogh, an African harp.

70 *Kitchen Table with Roast.* Oil, 50¾" × 28". Exhibited, Venice Biennale 1948.

71 A general view of his Paris studio; Braque at work. There is no cold north light; instead, the artist, through a system of curtains, can control the intensity of the sunlight. Braque constantly rearranges the position of his own works. There are several palettes in the room, several areas of work.

BRAQUE 64

BRAQUE 66

BRAQUE 67

A

B

C D

E F

G   H

I   J

K   L

BRAQUE

Continued

MASTERS OF CUBISM AND ABSTRACT ART

ANDINSKY   KUPKA   LARIONOV   GONTCHAROVA   BRANCUSI   LE CORBUSIER

KANDINSKY

Vassily Kandinsky is the first man who with paint and brush painted a non-representational work of art. Until that day in 1910 painting had to represent something; the artist communicated through recognizable and usually realistic subject matter. The grandeur of Kandinsky and the other pioneers of abstract art lies not in a new way of painting but in a new meaning given to the significance of work of art. Traditional art can be understood; at a glance one knows what the artist represents. This, truthfully, has always been but the superficial aspect of art; behind the great realistic masterpieces there always hides a higher meaning that raises the portrayal of reality into the realm of universal beauty and truth. This raising, this transposing of reality is, of course, a process of abstraction. Abstraction in art is not new; only the bad art never rose above itself and thus never achieved the dignity of a higher realm.

The revolution of Kandinsky's art is the making of abstraction itself the subject of the painting. In Kandinsky's memoirs he described the actual moment of the accidental discovery of non-representational or abstract art, when he was forty-four years old. Coming home at sunset from a session out of doors in 1910, his mind still absorbed by his work, he was struck as he entered his studio by an indescribably beautiful painting, all irradiated by an interior light." In the mysterious canvas he could distinguish only "forms and colors and no meaning." Suddenly he realized that it was one of his own paintings, turned on its side. "The next day in daylight I tried to recapture my previous impression. I only succeeded halfway. Even with the painting on its side, I could always find the object, but the blue light of dusk was missing. I knew then precisely that objects were harming my painting."

The thinking man of those days was torn between the unfathomable depths of his own inner world, as revealed by Freud, and the infinity of the universe of Einstein around him. It was as if the skin were the frontier of two universes receding from each other into boundless depths.

Man has known for centuries how his world of human beings, animals, trees, mountains, seas, rivers, and flowers has appeared to him. Suddenly one man, Kandinsky, stood up and, instead of facing outward from himself, turned and looked into himself.

Monet and the impressionists had disembodied reality by painting only its appearance as transformed through light and color. Van Gogh, the post-impres-

2 KANDINSKY

sionists, Matisse and the other *fauves,* with the emotional unreality of their col
transpositions had gone further in imposing over nature the artist's inner visio
Cézanne's attack on form, his rhythmic deformation of the human body, and tl
structural revelations of his still lifes and landscapes led directly to cubisı
Picasso and Braque followed Cézanne's teachings, and their many-faceted crysta
line explosions finally destroyed the myth of the sanctity of the object in art.

Each generation of painters had gone a step further than its predecesso
Once the object used as the subject of a painting was tampered with, distorted fo
purely pictorial reasons, it was inevitable that one day someone would throw tl
switch all the way over and make pictorial necessity "become the purpose of art
"The true subject of a picture is painting," said Kandinsky. His eye and min
were ready for the "accident" that was to start the abstract, non-objective, no
representational revolution that has dominated the art of our day.

Kandinsky, a Russian aristocrat with perhaps Mongol ancestors, deeply ir
bued with religious and cultural traditions, arrived, around 1900, in an ultr
civilized Germany where metaphysical and scientific searchings were flowerin
There a combination of Russian mysticism and Western aesthetics prepared hi
for the great discovery of non-objective art.

Wassily Kandinsky was born in Moscow on December 5, 1866. His paren
came from Siberia, that part of Russia that is in close contact with the Orien
Kandinsky studied law and political economy, and at twenty-three he went c
ethnological expeditions within Russia. He ended his scientific career at thirt
four when he decided to study painting in Germany. Kandinsky is a rare case
a great painter who came to art as a formed man, without having spent his you
in the study of art.

In 1914 at the outbreak of the war he returned to Russia, there to teach
the Moscow Academy of Fine Arts. After the Russian Revolution he went back
Germany, and in 1922 he joined the Bauhaus in Weimar, that creative scho
whose principal purpose was to find through art and technique the answer to tl
aesthetic demands of the modern world. For ten years he was a vital part of tha
extraordinary fertile international group of painters and architects: Lyon
Feininger, American; Paul Klee, Swiss; Kandinsky, Russian; Moholy-Nagy, Hu
garian; Walter Gropius, German. In 1932 Hitler closed the second, or Dessa
Bauhaus, and life for a free creative man became impossible in Germany. In 19!
Kandinsky went off to Paris to live there until his death on December 13, 1944,
the age of seventy-eight.

Throughout his life in Paris, Kandinsky and his wife, Nina, lived in an e
tremely modern apartment on the banks of the Seine in Neuilly. Madame Ka
dinsky, a frail, serious, attractive woman, still lives there.

There is no real studio in this apartment. The largest room, formerly
living room, was made into his workroom. Its walls are a medium gray. On
large desk-table next to the window there still is a typewriter, a crucifix, a ros
and neatly aligned pencils, knives, and pens. Several icons hang on one wal
Russian mysticism prevailing alongside a stark orderliness. There are sever
Russian peasant sculptures next to a Tanagra figurine. In front of the desk a
a gramophone and Kandinsky's armchair, covered with a sheet. No one had s
in it since his death.

Order, cleanliness, and method pervaded this room where Kandinsky worked during his ten years in Paris. Bottles, glasses, jars of colored powder are meticulously stacked and classified on shelves. Kandinsky mixed his own colors with a chemist's tools and a chemist's precision. Opaque white jars are lined up on their particular shelf, transparent jars on another shelf, next to glass retorts, white china crucibles, pharmaceutical flasks. Immaculate brushes are next to neatly stacked cartons of paints and columns of empty cigar and cigarette boxes which he used as miniature filing cabinets. On top of a bureau stands a glass vase filled with odd pieces of string, collected throughout the years.

Two large strikingly different canvases stood, the day I was there, on traditional brown wood easels. One was a 1906 pre-abstract landscape, the brilliant irregular areas of pure color clanging, as if through pure physical contact on the canvas a sound could be heard. Next to this image of passion was a serene geometric composition, *Two Green Dots,* painted in this studio. Here the artist created beauty not through passion, as in his earlier canvas, but through serene contemplation. The melodic unfolding of the composition makes the eye travel across the surface of the painting. In front of this Kandinsky painting the eye seems to listen. Kandinsky constantly surprises, caresses, charms, intrigues, purifies the experience of the eye. In each small area of the large canvas there is enough inventiveness to be the subject of a whole painting.

A door separated Kandinsky's work from everyday life. The entrance hall and the kitchen door were near his easel. He would have heard any ringing of the bell, any movement of a servant. But these intrusions did not seem to disturb him. Kandinsky knew exactly what he wanted to do with a painting; he visualized it before the very first sketch and rarely departed from his first inspiration. It was this security, this absolute control over his vision, which permitted Kandinsky to create among disturbing realities. A great self-confidence buttressed the security and the precision of Kandinsky's work.

Nina Kandinsky has a prodigious memory and an intense consciousness of her husband's greatness; they were married in 1916 and until his death they were never separated. She shared with him his constantly uprooted life and knows first-hand the intimate history of the birth of modern art.

"Kandinsky used to say," she said with a smile, "if it were up to the painters' wives to erect monuments, there wouldn't be any space left to move." Through her admiring description, the image of Kandinsky the man and the great artist merged. This was a unique unreeling of recollections and an intimate glimpse into the small details that make up the climate in which an artist's creative life develops.

"An aristocrat, an extremely sensitive man, always considerate of others and generous, Kandinsky could not stand anything Bohemian. For him Bohemia and all it stood for was just bad taste. He hated dirt, saying, 'I could paint in my white tie and tails.'

"He knew how to enjoy things, the way children and the pure in heart do. He could laugh until he cried. He always seemed the youngest in any group. He radiated optimism and great wisdom, but above all he knew how to communicate his strength to others. He saw the positive in everything.

"His daily timetable was leisurely. He would get up at nine, take a bath, then breakfast. This was the sacred moment of the day. From eleven A.M. to twelve thirty P.M., work in the studio, then a walk along the Seine. He needed the con stant presence of nature.

"He, the abstract painter, would say, 'Now I can love nature even more. do not see it any longer as a model; I admire it and just enjoy it.'

"Lunch was at one o'clock; if tired by the morning's work, he read detectiv novels. After lunch, rest; then a Russian tea and more work in the studio unti dusk. He liked to have friends for dinner, but hated unexpected guests. Afte dinner he would draw and read; Dickens especially calmed him.

"Sometimes he listened to the radio or played his records. Music was alway his principal relaxation, especially symphonic compositions. As a youth he ha studied music; he could play the piano and the 'cello. His favorite composers wer Beethoven, Bach, Moussorgsky, Stravinsky, Prokofiev.

"When he went out he liked only the good restaurants.

"His years at the Bauhaus were happy ones. There his friendship with tha other great master of modern art, Paul Klee, developed; Klee an introvert, Kan dinsky an extrovert. When the press attacked the Bauhaus and Kandinsky's ar Klee came and looked at the abstract *Composition VIII* and said, 'It is a thing o genius.' Kandinsky knew that an artist should find a lesson in the public's lack o understanding. 'I am very happy that abstract art is not recognized; it is a sig of strength.'

"Deep in himself Kandinsky, who spent the major part of his life outsid Russia, felt always Russian. He was stamped for life by his childhood memories o ancient Moscow with its walled Kremlin, hundreds of Byzantine churches, and th exuberant unbridled fantasy of its Oriental Slav architecture. The roots of hi art are in the Russian icons, the religious images of the orthodox faith. He wa religious, but he seldom went to church. 'Strange that there are people who d not believe!' he would say."

In his youth in Russia, he saw a Monet painting of a haystack. "I had th impression that here painting was, in a certain way, the subject of the paintin and I asked myself if one could not go much further in the same direction. Afte that I looked at Russian icons with new eyes, that is to say, that I had eyes fo what was abstract in art."

In his prophetic book *The Art of Spiritual Harmony,* in 1912, he wrot "The salvation of art and of man is a spiritual one. One does not have to pain Madonnas to be a religious painter." When in 1911 the "Blue Rider" group, whic included Kandinsky, Macke, and Marc, was founded in Munich, they believe in a "new Renaissance, an inner one." The only law of the artist is his "inne necessity." Kandinsky proclaimed the "absolute freedom" of the artist. He adde "Such spiritual freedom is as necessary in art as it is in life."

But abstraction, being the mirror of the artist's soul, shows up his inne quality. Abstract art demands higher standards of the artist himself. In a ba realistic picture there is always the consolation of reproduced reality; in a ba abstraction there is either the frustration of a purely decorative experience, painted by an artist who has nothing to express, or the shocking evidence, u hidden by traces of pleasing reality, of a lack of spiritual value.

Abstract art has been, and is, misunderstood. It is condemned as a meanin less, destructive attack on all that is sacred and beautiful. The tragedy of this misconception is that abstract art in its highest form is an expression of man's desire to call upon the highest aspirations that he intuitively feels, to rise above subject matter into a higher realm which, like a prayer, will call upon his spiritual energy. Kandinsky's new vision of art was "something that appeals less to the eye and more to the soul."

He believed that music is the supreme art, that every creator, in whatever field, must learn the methods of music to apply them to his own medium. He described music as "the best teacher . . . the art which has devoted itself not to the reproduction of actual phenomena but to the expression of the artist's soul."

For paintings to achieve the same effect, the lessons of music had to be studied and applied. The laws of harmony, rhythm, composition, transposed into pictorial language, would lead man through painting into the highest forms of art. "Color is the keyboard, the eyes are the harmonies, the soul is the piano with many strings."

For the spectator the way to abstract art is through an emotional reaction. Between the painting and the onlooker a bond of sympathy and attraction has to exist. One must literally fall in love with a painting. This by-passing of the intellect is a direct appeal to feeling. Logic, understanding, cannot prove everything, but emotion, by upsetting our contact with reality, can put us into a state where without proof we are willing to believe.

Abstract art is an attempt at direct communication with the spectator, a search for an instinctive response in the onlooker, unspoiled by preconceived, hard-to-dispose-of associations. To search for meaning in an abstract painting is to try to open a door with a wrong key. Meaning is there, but not a meaning that is translatable into words. Kandinsky said, "When something appears senseless, and people say, 'It does not mean anything,' this must not be interpreted literally. There isn't a form, there isn't a thing in the world that means nothing." There are in our lives moments of indescribable emotion; words fail us many times; this vision beyond the describable is the realm of non-representational art.

Those who protest against the lack of meaning in abstract art would be hard put to describe the soul in words. That spirit, that soul, has its own laws.

How can an artist find out the aesthetic demands of his soul? Only by subjecting each creative motion to the laws of his inner necessity. That necessity is the artist's own inner constant; he is what he is, he feels the way he feels because of that inner control. Too few creators dare to listen to this supreme command.

These simple words of Kandinsky's are his final summation, the lesson of his life and art, rules for the inspired creative artist: "Do not fall into a manner. Change; find by yourself and do not copy, make it your own."

NOTES ON THE ILLUSTRATIONS

Wassily Kandinsky. 1866–1944. Born, Russia.
Photographs taken in 1954.

72 *Water color on a black background,* 1940. 19⅜″ × 12⅝″. Collection Rupf, Bern.

73 In Kandinsky's Paris studio, next to his paintbrushes, Russian wooden toy sculpture, a nostalgic link with his childhood.

74 Kandinsky's Paris studio, as he left it at his death in 1944. On an easel next to his carefully arranged painting cabinet, which he called "my keyboard," stands a large serene composition, *Two Green Dots,* painted in 1935. The two oils under glass, done in 1911, are among the first abstract paintings. The photograph on the wall is of Kandinsky, taken in 1933.

KUPKA

"Renaissance. That's macaroni. . . .
"I prefer Rodin to Michelangelo."

A slight, very thin, very wrinkled man with pale blue-gray eyes spoke. His skin, like yellow parchment, shriveled into a multitude of crisscrossed lines over sunken cheeks and protruding cheekbones. His collar hung loosely around his gaunt, bird-like neck. His gnarled hands moved quickly and, when he spoke, his eyes closed and he pursed his lips, sucking in his wasted cheeks. This Czech with the Mongol traits of Middle Europe made one think of a Buddhist priest. Against his pale eyes, his white hair, his pale blue-gray suit, the only contrasting accent was the red rosette of the Legion of Honor.

This iconoclastic, withered old man of eighty-three was Frank Kupka, one of the fathers of abstract art. His wife stood protectively near him, her massive earthy frame a contrast to his frail elongated body. In her dark peasant features traces of beauty remained. She had posed for Renoir.

The dining-room windows of their Puteaux house opened onto a curious artists' community: an overgrown suburban plot surrounded by low buildings, dark and dilapidated like abandoned pavilions, in which lived some of the most creative artistic thinkers of our day: the Duchamp-Villon brothers, and the Kupkas. This was the "Puteaux Group."

The Kupkas lived in the same house for forty-six years. When they first moved in the rent was 800 francs a year; the region was infested with bandits, and meals were safer with revolvers on the table. Madame Kupka recalls that they were so poor that the big nude Kupka exhibited in the Salon on the Champs Elysées she herself carted in a pushcart all the way from Puteaux to the Salon, a distance of about eight kilometers. When Kupka needed canvas for her portrait she had to rip the cover of her mattress. She tried to hide their poverty from her husband. When he had an attack due to alcoholism she saved him from the insane asylum because she knew that there he could not paint. She treated him tenderly like a child, and said with pride and self-pity, "He is my son."

Kupka rose every morning at seven. For breakfast she cooked him pancakes with jam. He loved to eat and to drink and had fish and meat twice a day. Our luncheon, prepared by Madame herself, was typical. We had lobster, vegetable salad, eggs mayonnaise, roast chicken with new potatoes, string beans, salad, cheese, wild strawberries, chocolate mousse, fruit; and with succeeding courses white wine, Pommard, and liqueurs.

After lunch we went upstairs. Here, after the cramped, crowded smallness of the dining room, was a huge studio two stories high—as big as the whole house. As with other painters, everything seemed sacrificed for the one glorious room which was the mainstay of life.

The studio was sad. Its walls were gray. On the floor lay a rug with black and white swirling patterns of Kupka's own design. Some of the furniture was Chinese, and the whole decorative feeling of the room was a gaudy reminder of the *art nouveau* style. In his early work now hanging on the walls this painter had been a severe academic realist. He had evolved slowly away from realistic portraits, preoccupied by the mystery of the prismatic breaking of light. He abandoned impressionistic bathers with *fauve* accents for a new world of geometry and space. Rhythmic variations, themes and fugues, the harmonious movement of form and color became the basis of his art. Although dusty books and papers littered his desk, although many of the studio's furnishings seemed terribly dated, a new canvas in progress on his easel was the work of a young man. It was intense, clean, and vibrant.

Kupka spoke of painting. His definition: "Painting is the visual pleasure of a thing well organized, constructed in beautiful color."

He insisted that art must be clean and one's work must be clean.

"Color must be frank. Shading is weakening. Everything must be precision. When one crosses a street all our acts are dictated by precision. It is through our precise movements that we avoid death and accident.

"In the old days no one looked closely at painting; now it is examined very, very closely, so it must be precise. Paint cleanly.

"Mysticism in painting does not lead anywhere. Optical research does not lead anywhere. One does not have to be inspired by forms of nature. One must turn one's back on nature—everything is in the head, the mind."

Kupka was very critical of his own work; he disliked anything he painted and wanted to rework or destroy it. He painted after many, many studies, taking infinite pains, redrawing in pastels the original inspiration before putting it down on canvas.

"Goncourt has said one needs nine years to create a book, and I say one needs six years for a good painting."

About exhibitions, Kupka remarked, "To exhibit, why? So that everyone can copy you?"

His culture and memory were incredible. His favorite reading was astronomy and Plato. All philosophy fascinated him. He knew and he followed everything that happened in the world around him.

He often fell into long, deep silences; suddenly his eyes would fill with tears when some inner thought welled up within him. He said, "It's terrible for a painter to go blind." At the age of eighty-three, just as the public and the museums were beginning to recognize him, his eyesight began to fail, and in the last years of his life he painted with great difficulty.

Kupka and his wife sacrificed everything in life for their belief in his art. He was a pioneer, misunderstood, unrecognized. He felt bitter that many who had come after him grew famous and wealthy and that he, one of the early innovators had been by-passed. When visitors came to see his more famous contemporary Villon, who lives in the house farther down in the garden, they walked by the Kupka house; and these two proud people could see famous art dealers and visiting celebrities stalk by their house, pretending that they did not know them. The art dealers were, as Kupka said, waiting for him to die. He paid the price of having been many years ahead of his time. Neglected, alone, unrecognized, these two old people strove to finish their lives with the one hope that all of their sacrifices might not have been in vain.

The Kupkas were married for over forty years. Theirs was the most striking example of a painter's ménage. The wife lived for her husband. She had sacrificed her life, her interests—everything for her husband-child. She believed in him and she would do anything to help him achieve success. She had the will to save him as she had saved him from the insane asylum; she had the will to save him from any misery, she hid any suffering that might hamper his peace of mind or his creativeness. Today his success and vindication are justifications of her own life.

Kupka lived through this life sheltered and protected as though in a dream, in communion with his philosophers, his ideas, his research; like a composer he had to work logically, slowly, methodically, and he needed this peace, this divorce from the worries of everyday existence. When one saw the Kupkas one realized what it meant to devote one's life to an ideal, to brave solitude, misery, nonrecognition, and to struggle on despite them.

Many have died without ever knowing any recognition at all. Kupka died just before knowing that his name in the history of art and his place in the abstract century are secure. His was a desperate striving for a new horizon, a search to give the world a new visual experience.

NOTES ON THE ILLUSTRATIONS

Frank Kupka. 1871–1957. Born, Czechoslovakia.
Photographs taken in 1949, 1953, 1956.

75 Woodcut from *Quatre Histoires de Blanc et Noir,* 1926.

76 Kupka in 1952 seated in his Puteaux studio. Next to a realistic bust of his wife stands a first study for his *Fugue Chromatique,* one of the first nonobjective paintings.

77 The painting side of his studio. The large, mysterious early Kupka, second from left, contrasts with the more definite, precise paintings of his late period.

78 Kupka a year before his death, standing in front of one of his great early abstract masterpieces. Dressed in soiled white, he raised his arms in an all embracing prophetic gesture, an unforgettable vision of speechless desire for expression.

LARIONOV AND GONTCHAROVA

n Moscow in 1911, the name *rayonnism* was invented by Michael Larionov to lescribe his and his wife's near-abstract pictures, composed of raylike lines. These rtists settled in Paris in 1914, brought there by Diaghilev, whose ballets had remendous impact on the cultural life of the French capital. The judgment of oosterity has caught up with these pioneers. They are a living lesson of the pa- ience that sometimes the greatest artists need in order to experience recognition.

For about fifty years Nathalie Gontcharova and Michael Larionov have ived in the same apartment and studio. They preserve an extraordinary human elationship, treating each other with the ceremonial tenderness of members of ome secret order. Now in their old age, they speak softly and move with diffi- :ulty. Larionov's bold humor is counterpoint to the aristocratic calm of his wife.

NOTES ON THE ILLUSTRATIONS

Michael Larionov. 1881–1964. Nathalie Gontcharova. 1881–1962. Both born, Russia. Photographs taken in 1950, 1952.

79 The two great artists on one of their now rare visits to their Rue Visconti studio. In the background, two early Larionov paintings: left, realistic *The Barber;* right, cubist *Landscape.*

80 They live in a small two-room apartment next to the École des Beaux-Arts, in the center of the Left Bank. An unbelievable accumulation of books, art documents, paintings, and drawings reaches to the ceilings, crowding and restricting movement.

BRANCUSI

'or years I tried to photograph him, but toward the end of his life he had a super- tition that if his picture were taken he would die. I sat opposite him many times, ny camera on my lap, not daring to transgress his command. "Why do you want o photograph me? I am old. My works are my portrait. They are my children. . . Don't write down what I am saying. I don't like fame. I have known fame. 'm sorry I'm not a bum singing near subway entrances. I love to sing; I even nake up rhymes."

Brancusi's great studio was in the Impasse Ronsin not far from Montparnasse. Iuddled around it was a cluster of studios, all doomed by the encroaching city. They seemed like a medieval village clinging for protection to the Brancusi castle. Only his fame kept the demolition squads away. And only a thin battered door orotected him from the outside; his tiny living quarters off the studio opened lirectly into an unpaved alley.

There was a mattress on the bare floor; there was a two-burner gas stove; and ll around, the clutter of discarded sculpture, tools, plaster casts, wood carved and uncarved, marble, and many withered bouquets of flowers kept, curiously, like love fetishes. On the whitewashed walls hung his sculpture tools, fantastic shapes, rusty, black, and ominous as the instruments of a medieval torture chamber. Pointing to them, he said, "This is my arsenal."

Even though he was ill, the room was cold. No one was around to serve or help him, but suspended over his bed was a huge brass disk that he could strike if he needed help from his neighbor-friends. "The doctor told me recently to go for a useful walk. So, I go out and get my food. What could be more useful?"

As he sat up in bed, motionless, now silent but still aggressive and proud, he created a strange aura of wisdom and magic. He made me think of a Buddhist monk and of Merlin the magician. His pale yellow skin, his long, unkempt white beard, pointed knitted skull cap, and once-white bathrobe, all added to my feeling that he belonged to no definite period, that he was outside of time and history. Through the narrow slits of his eyelids his pale, piercing eyes glistened, shrewd eyes that accented the biting intensity of his words. He spoke as if he wanted his words to cut through thought as his hands cut through marble. All the wisdom of the world seemed on the edge of his tongue. The mysteries of Egypt, of China, and of the Bible were always present in his thoughts. It was as if he had been where no one else dared go.

Once while he cooked his own lunch he said, "We live off manna. There is a layer of manna on which we feed. We think that we are warmed by the sun, but that is false. The sun is going to perish. From time to time I even see the ions when they light up. They light up when the sun is perpendicular to the Equator. The sky that men believe to be blue is not. It is black beyond."

When he relaxed, Lao-tse was spiritually near him. "Lao-tse wanted to find out why little animals seem happy. He watched them and realized that the secret was play. They play all the time. To live long, do as the little animals—play."

We had many long talks, and here are some of the things he told me.

"I was born in the mountains of Rumania. My father gave me tsuika to drink when I was two and a half. He used to drink and beat me and put horse dung under my nose. He wanted a daughter. . . .

"It is because of a violin that I came to sculpture. I was eleven years old, working in a cleaning and dyeing shop. I had straightened out and arranged everything so well in the shop that the owner said to me, 'I know something you will not be able to do—make a violin.' I started working and made a violin. I discovered the secret of Stradivarius. I hollowed out the wood, I boiled it. The violin made a wonderful sound. After I made the violin, the owner said, 'You must be a sculptor.' . . .

"I started school, jumped several classes, then got a scholarship to the art school. I finished at the Beaux-Arts with three diplomas. I studied anatomy and made a sculpture of the musculature of a man. It is still used by students. To do it I had to dissect more than a hundred cadavers. . . .

"Once I was asked to create a monument to a dead poet. One of the figures was a woman. All of a sudden she looked too real to me. I felt like handling her roughly. I wanted to express prayer . . . when the arms are crossed. Then the woman looked as though she was cold. I cut off the arms. I understood then that realism was not essential to expression. . . .

"I came to Paris in 1904, practically on foot. Paris was beautiful, 'La Belle Époque.' There were no automobiles. At first I washed glasses in a café. The Queen of Rumania wanted me to study with Rodin. I said, 'Nothing ever grows under great trees. Why do you want to smother me?'. . .

"I worked with wood because it was cheaper than marble. Marble was one hundred francs a kilo. I don't like the veins in marble. I want anonymity. Then, too, marble dust penetrates all. I've tried everything, even masks, but still it penetrates into you through the pores. . . .

"The bird—I am always working on it. I have not yet found it. It is not a bird, it is the meaning of flight. . . .

"Over there is a turtle, a turtle that flies. It is the material that dictates to us our creation. The marble did not allow for legs. In that other corner is a turtle that crawls, made of wood. . . .

"I do not follow what is happening in art movements. When one finds his own direction, he is so busy that there is no time.

"Why have pupils? One cannot teach soul. For them everything has to be prepared on a conveyor belt. Then one is not free any more if he feels like doing something. Young arists see things from the outside. They see the surface. One must forget what one learns. . . .

"To see far is one thing, to get there is something else.

"Intelligence helps us if we give it the brakes of love and soul. Nowadays everyone is intelligent. It is a bad thing. Intelligence is fictitious. Love is spiritual, it is the Divine. Physical love means emptying oneself. Real love is God. The soul is everything. To make love gives us a glimpse of the Divine. . . .

"No religion. I was an archdeacon in my church. I took things from Jesus Christ. Love each other. Rid yourself of evil. Save your soul. If you live well, if you purify yourself, you go up into the heavens and stay there. If you live badly you come back onto this earth or another earth. Earth is a hell.

"I have been in Egypt and visited the tombs of the Pharaohs. I even went as far as Aden. . . .

"In India it has been proved that there were ten or eleven deluges, although we know of only one. We are living the beginning of a new apocalypse. The deluge is coming. Nothing will be saved. Sculpture will be lost in the sand. . . .

"If one could create as one breathes. That would be true happiness. One should arrive at that."

Once while I was with him, this very old sage, withered and seemingly weak, got up suddenly, opened an extraordinary all-wood door he had carved himself, and went into his hangarlike studio. He decided that a monumental sculpture was out of place and with incredible, unexpected power pushed it into the desired place. I will never forget the image of that small, gray, bent figure shuffling and limping through the maze of sky-reaching sculptures he had charged with the eternal energy-giving powers of art.

NOTES ON THE ILLUSTRATIONS

Constantin Brancusi. 1876–1957. Born, Rumania.
Photographs taken in 1955.

81 The mysteriously ornamented sliding door that separates Brancusi's living quarters from the studio. Recognizable sculptures are on the left: a plaster enlargement of *The Cock;* next to it, one of several versions of *Bird in Space,* and, standing majestically in the center, the wood *King of Kings.*

82 Inside a vast plaster shell, a rare Brancusi painting, *Flying Bird,* and under it, a polished bronze head of a child.

83 A view of one side of the immense studio, taken while Brancusi was alive, with its fantastic accumulation of forms. On the right, the giant versions of *The Cock.* A smaller plaster version is on its stand in front of the painted backdrop. On the left of it is *The Blond Negress.* In the left foreground, one of Brancusi's early works, *The Kiss.* In his testament he left the whole studio and its contents to the French government on condition that the studio be reconstructed exactly as it was in his lifetime.

LE CORBUSIER

Le Corbusier lives and works on the top floor of one of the first ultra-modern apartment houses that he designed in Paris. His studio, with the main wall of rough-textured stone and the ceiling vaulted, gives the feeling of an unfinished chapel. The large paintings with their bright yet strangely soft colors contrast startlingly with the monastic cement and stone. Le Corbusier himself is a man of contrasts. The formal bow tie he was wearing was out of place with his short sleeved shirt. He is businesslike, distant, and severe. He creates on as grand a scale as any artist in history, yet there in his studio the sketches and paintings seem small, like initial images in his mind, fertile cells ready for growth. In contrast to them were hundreds of paint cans arranged subconsciously by the great architect-painter in front of his easel on the floor to resemble a visionary city as if seen from the air. To this austere master all form and space seem to be rough, disorganized materials which are in need of discipline.

NOTES ON THE ILLUSTRATION

Le Corbusier (Charles-Édouard Jeanneret). 1887–1965. Born, Switzerland. Photograph taken in 1954.

84 Le Corbusier at work in front of his easel. A founder, with Ozenfant, o purism in the early twenties. Painting has always been a secret backbone o his art. He has continued to paint and sculpt while erecting one of the great est architectural visions of our time. Throughout history, some of the greates architects have been painters and sculptors, and some of the great painter and sculptors have been architects: Giotto, Michelangelo, Da Vinci, and L Corbusier.

75

KUPKA

KUPKA 78

LARIONOV AND GONTCHAROVA

82

BRANCUSI

Continued

MASTERS OF CUBISM AND ABSTRACT ART

LÉGER   VILLON   DUCHAMP   PEVSNER   ARP

LÉGER

For more than thirty years Fernand Léger lived on a sunny, quiet street in Paris near the Luxembourg Gardens. A tall neoclassic portal opened onto the narrow courtyard of his house, two floors of which Léger used for his studio and another for his apartment. An incredibly narrow, winding wooden staircase led up to the first landing, where a sign announced that all appointments had to be made through the secretary of M. Léger. If, however, the visitor knew Léger, it was all right to go straight up. The stairs were so steep that I arrived out of breath. Léger opened the door. In a gruff voice he said, "Come in. Oh, hello. It's you."

I found myself in an immense double-storied room. With the strong light softened by sliding white curtains, a sensation of overwhelming color came from the red, paint-spattered floor and from the kaleidoscopic far wall covered from ceiling to floor with his own paintings. The intensity of colors and lines combined to create an instant vibration. Léger wore a checked shirt, and the violent pattern of his clothes against the violent pattern of his paintings made him seem like a chameleon. This mimetic camouflage between Léger and the art that he had created was not only superficial; the forms on the canvases of nudes, acrobats, and bicyclists also resembled the massive form of their creator.

Léger was heavily built, rough-hewn. His face consisted of powerful lines and volumes, shaped like the limbs of the figures he painted. The extraordinary deep furrows, the wrinkles on his brow, the two deep-set lines on each side of his nose, the lines under his eyes, all dug deep into the massive face. One vertical line cut his forehead in two even parts. I thought of the Byzantine icons with their harshly outlined features. His eyes and mouth, like slits in a mask, seemed small in his big, mobile, symmetrical, primitive face. I thought, too, of the weather-ravaged features of peasants and laborers in the out-of-doors.

When he smiled, a tenderness softened his somewhat brutal features. There was great heartiness in his manner, his laughter, his jokes. He had a spontaneity of gesture and a need for communication with the world. The telephone rang frequently, and he had a gruff familiarity with people on the phone, with me, with visiting students. In spite of his massiveness, he had a surprising lightness in action. When he spoke, his hands darted quickly, his supple fingers bending expressively. I felt an immediate friendship for him. He picked up a drawing and said, "I will autograph it for you as a souvenir of your visit."

This feeling of spontaneity, of generosity, was visible in Léger's actual palette.

85 LÉGER

On it colors were two or three inches thick. Vigorously, abundantly squeezed ou the colors formed miniature mountains. From the constant rubbing of the brush colored peaks had been hollowed into craters, the reminders of creative eruption.

Next to this extraordinary palette stood a folding stepladder. On each step there were brushes—an inventive solution for the problem of storage. Behind the brush stand was a long mirror. In it Léger could look at his paintings from a distance. For him the relationship between the dimension of the work of art and the space around it was all-important. He remarked that this Paris studio was eight meters long and six meters wide, the perfect proportion, adding, "I am a victim of dimension."

The floor of his studio was unique. Most artists in their studios surround themselves with monochromatic or subdued color, but the deep red floor of Léger's studio was an intense base from which his eye received a constant shock. He needed the stimulus of pure color. The blotting papers on his writing table under the window were red, yellow, green—bright and intense.

I had expected Léger to be surrounded with elements from the modern mechanical civilization, but his studio was bare of inspirational objects. I looked at his recent canvases, filled with the memories of his childhood in Normandy, cows, roosters, country-fair musicians playing the accordion, acrobats, bicyclists, men and women enjoying life's simplest pastimes and relaxations. I realized that Léger no longer sought his chief inspiration in industrial or agricultural machines. I sensed a reaction against the mechanical—against abstraction per se. "Abstraction, that's good for the decorative," he exclaimed. A return to the human, to nature was now foremost in his mind. He wanted to reassure through the use of the familiar.

A short while before his death, as if to satisfy this need for nature, his rediscovered source of inspiration, he bought an abandoned inn at Gif, in the Vallée de Chevreuse, the tender, undulating countryside that flanks Paris. There, surrounded by farms, but within quick reach of the city, he spent his last months. Gradually he abandoned Paris for the studio in Gif, a former ballroom which he quickly filled with the gay color beat of his last major work, *La Grande Parade.* This gigantic canvas of circus figures blocked off one whole wall, as if Léger wanted to impress upon the art of easel painting a new grandeur, a fresh concept of monumentality.

Great architecture has always tended toward the monumental, and Léger followed this trend. "When a thing is powerful it is not fragile," he said. Largeness of conception, a feeling of volume and scale, a generosity and abundance of form characterize his later work.

At the opposite end of the studio, facing this enormous circus panorama, stood a very large black and white porcelain bas-relief. Léger often sat under it when tired, in a colored deck chair to contemplate his work from a distance. While he sat in this chair, talking to me, a steady stream of recollection poured forth. As if hypnotized by his own art, he seemed to dig into the innermost layers of consciousness. "I am a Norman. I'm a primitive. My father was a cattle dealer. I went into painting instead of beef. As a child I never drew. Around sixteen or seventeen I did some caricatures, some sculptures out of chestnuts."

Suddenly, he looked around him and exclaimed with wonderment, "How ould I have become a painter with all that cattle running over me? I am a child of the earth, of the Norman earth, and I am proud of it!

"To earn my living I became a photographic retoucher and did photomontage. Maybe it is true that the smooth gray shading in my paintings comes from that training. Then I became a draftsman in an architect's office, but I always painted on the side. I was in utter misery. I didn't have a cent. It is only very late that recognition came. . . . The French like impressionists.

"Braque and Picasso are impressionists. I, never! Their mandolins were selling when my pistons were laughed at. Impressionism is sensuality."

I asked him who were his great influences: "Cézanne, Douanier, Rousseau. Rousseau taught me the quality of finish—he used to say to me, 'Monsieur Léger, why doesn't Monsieur Matisse finish?'

"I was very fond of the Douanier. I'll tell you an amusing incident. The Douanier wanted to exhibit in the official Salon but he was refused. With some of my friends, I arranged for the Salon des Indépendants to hang his paintings. But the Douanier, being a real civil servant, wanted official recognition. So when the Minister of the Beaux-Arts came to inaugurate the Indépendants, the frustrated Douanier ran up to me and said, 'Monsieur Léger, is it the same minister as in the official Salon?'

"Wars have always had a determining influence on my life. In the First World War, I was an engineer. There and then I had contact with the reality and the solidity of life. The breech of a seventy-five-millimeter cannon has taught me more than museums. I saw the magnitude of the machine and the antlike smallness of man.

"But I came into contact, too, with the People with a capital P, and that was the truly deciding influence on my life. I got to know them, to love them and their language, so direct, so full of imagery. The simple people have real instinct. For example"—he smiled—"an elegant woman wears a pink sash; a woman of the people would wear a red sash. Taste is the enemy of painting."

The Second World War exiled Léger to America; that was his second visit. The years spent in the most modern of civilizations stamped his work indelibly, but curiously made him seek the human element.

"I remember a man standing on Broadway," he said. "The lights kept changing and he seemed lit up, as if abstracted by the reflections of the neon lights. He would suddenly turn from red to green. There the idea of color outside of the drawn image came to me. And the idea of bodies hurling through space came to me on a crowded American beach where I saw sixty or eighty people simultaneously diving, jumping.

"You see, I earn my life on the roads. My eyes are on life. I pick up everything. I even have a television set; on it I pick up deformation.

"I make notations in contact with nature, but create from memory. I hate abstraction and those horrible abstractionists. I went through an abstract period but only to bury it better."

He stopped for a moment, then mused, "All the things that go through one's head and that one doesn't fulfill."

There was a silence. Then he added, "Cézanne did not fulfill.

"Artists are divided into two groups, the classicists and the romantics. The classicists are the men of the North. They are slower. Picasso is an example of the romantic, a precocious child of the South, for in the South men awaken to life earlier. I build, I am a Norman. I am a classicist. I am at peace with myself. My torment and suffering are purely aesthetic. I don't philosophize; I just paint paint, paint.

"The great primitives, like Giotto, are my masters. In their art the subject is second to plastic values. They had plastic liberty. There must be plastic freedom They used color arbitrarily. Colors in an object are imprisoned. One must not submit to the subject. My main preoccupation is with the question of color inside form or outside of it."

Around the room were several canvases, drawings, gouaches of the circus. Some of the "circus parades" were realistically colored with a three-dimensional effect like magnificent *images d'épinal;* others showed how, step by step, Léger liberated color from form.

It was an extraordinary experience to be present when a great painter struggled to make up his mind. The conflict between realism and abstraction tormented Léger to his last day. Side by side, he had two large canvases of his circus. In one the color was used realistically, filling in the forms prescribed by his black outline. It was a beautiful work. The sky was blue, the clown's nose red, all colors had their predestined place. But somehow there was no mystery; the viewer's mind rested, unstimulated by the expected; there was no surprise to free one's imagination by disconnecting it from its habitual manner of thinking.

The mystery of the unexpected, the surprise of incongruous juxtaposition generate a friction in our brains, giving off the spark that imagination yearns for. Léger, as he contemplated his realistic circus parade, felt the lack of this vital stimulation. He made up his mind then that form and color must be free of each other, and painted his final *Grande Parade* with the liberated color playing over the interweaving images of dancers, acrobats, clowns, and horses. This, his last work, was his masterpiece and his testament. He had solved his conflict. "This way, with the color outside, there is a double play and a double effect."

In his painting Léger attempted to satisfy the visual needs of human beings just as modern architects seek to solve their physical demands. The great architects of the past consciously created sensory effects on the spectator by leading him, for example, from a narrow passage into a vast hall. Léger created the same spatial feeling of mental expansion or contraction by juxtaposing seemingly contradictory scales. As I looked at the canvases around me, I realized that a painting by Léger was fundamentally an imaginary architectural rendering. Objects and people were studied like the elevation and plans of buildings.

On the immense canvas in front of us, the bold, black, sinuous outlines of the figures were independent of the circles, squares, and triangles of pure color. Simplified areas of color clarified the whole pictorial concept, as an architectural master plan clearly expresses its dominant themes. Léger's color was seen as if hovering above the surface of the painting and looking down. But the figures drawn in black lines over this color were seen from a different point of view— from the side, in elevation, the way we normally see buildings and human beings. This double play on our senses creates an unexpected sensation. We never stop to think that we live and walk over vast plans of cities, of buildings; in act, we forget the existence of such plans and are conscious only of verticals.

The big, gruff man covered his eyes with his hands and leaned back in the deck chair. Then, after a pause, he summed up, "My purpose is to give certitude in art." After a few moments' silence, he got up with an effort, and we went into the sunlit countryside. The garden furniture had been painted bright red, yellow, blue; it stood out against the whitewashed walls. Under a widespread tree hung a mobile and a plastic acid-green watering hose which added a completely contemporary accent. But the roof was of centuries-old tile. Léger, in a green-belted hunter's vest, touched the low-hanging tiles lovingly. For an instant he seemed transported into his childhood. Proud of his tiles, he looked at me, shrugged his shoulders, and smiled, saying, "I am a Norman." He had just married his second wife, a Russian who had worked with him twenty-five years in his art school. "I said to myself, 'What will become of me, old and alone?' " Léger continued, "Love and painting are two very different things. To make love tires one. The artist is an egoist. No woman has had a hold on me. Only painting has counted in my life."

The key to his art was the audience he sought. "Everyday people . . . I love them . . . their language, so direct. . . ."

Of all the modern masters, he was the one most conscious of the present world of machines, industry, speed, the world of advertising, of the quick, direct appeal to the spectators' senses. Magazines, newspapers, television, movies, posters use attention-getting devices that are part of our everyday life. They have been carefully separated from so-called fine art. But basically there is no division. A poster can be art. Many people, forgetting the long history of art, often think, carelessly, that only a framed object with three-dimensional shading and perspective is a painting, and that a bright-colored flat surface is decoration or advertising.

Advertising, the graphic arts, considered apart from painting, have the secret of mass appeal. Toulouse-Lautrec, the impressionists, Bonnard, and others enriched their paintings from the art of the poster. Scientific investigation of human reactions, the probing of psychological research into human vision, and the investigation of the subconscious by psychoanalysis have given to the graphic artist invaluable data. Traditional art relied on intuition to achieve universal appeal and ignored the revolution in our knowledge about ourselves, our likes, our dislikes. It ignored the scientific discoveries of perception. Art became really modern art when all this accumulation of knowledge became part of the creative artists' means of expression. Modern art is the visible acknowledgment of mankind's awakening to itself. Cubism, surrealism, abstraction are not manners or ways of painting; they are signs of artistic maturity, the affirmation of artistic freedom from the superstitious worship of tradition.

One of the discoveries of modern psychology is that for intensification of vision our eyes demand contrast. Contrast is the basic law of advertising. Léger more than others used this knowledge of contrast in his art to achieve a direct, deep physical reaction. He re-established the value of the sign, the essential time-saving symbol of communication.

It is rewarding to think of art as primarily communication between the artist and the spectator. One of the purposes of cybernetics, the science of communication, is that there be no loss, waste, confusion, or distortion in the message conveyed. In his use of thick, bold, precise outline, Léger sought to reduce the area of misinterpretation or error. Speaking of line, he said, "Line is everything. What would my art be without that black line?" His line is not the refined, sensuous vibrating line of the traditional master draftsman. It is the line which, like writing, defines precise vision and thought. Directness of response to his work was one of his goals. "I believe in painting that hooks one!" he said.

Until modern art, paintings had to be penetrated by the spectator. Léger paintings reach out to the observer. In our day one sees so many visual images that their individual impression can be easily dulled. Léger's aggressive conception has given art a commanding new voice. His paintings do not require participation and response that our distracted minds cannot give.

If you enter a room in which there are several paintings by different artists a Léger will probably attract your eye first. This bombardment of our sensitivity is in harmony with contemporary visual thinking. His is not an art in which the spectator tries to escape and forget reality in a dream world of pleasant images. His is an art that aggressively knocks on our senses, forcing us to recognize it. If it does bring joy and beauty, it is not through escape.

Léger was squarely planted in the midst of our civilization. He was not preoccupied with the Etruscans or with African sculpture. His was the world of today and of tomorrow. And his influence may be the greatest on the generation to come, because he was not afraid to make art without art. Our century is obsessed with the idea of work. Léger faced the aesthetic problem of the working man in his series of builders; his men at work are great odes to human progress. He respected human beings who build. Of himself he said, "I build." There was nothing destructive in Léger's art. On the contrary, there was a constant glorification of the means and materials through which creativeness is made possible: the hands of the workers, their gloves, trousers, caps, their tools, the scaffolding, the girders, the rivets, the machines.

He wanted to stop the ever-increasing division between art and life. He wanted to bridge this gulf by the use of permanent symbols. His was a dual return to the human, in the subject matter of his art and in the methods he used to act on the spectator. In his subject matter he rediscovered for himself the human form. In his methods he used the lessons taught by modern psychology. Léger's art may seem crude to the sophisticated; it is a warning to return to the basic instincts that motivate the human race. He believed in art for the many, not art for the few. Like the great religious primitive Giotto, he wanted to satisfy the humble and the great, the peasant and the intellectual.

Maybe art in its preoccupation with aesthetics and ornamentation has lost contact with its primeval impetus. Returning to the human form, Léger had perhaps reasoned, was one of the surest ways to re-establish art's universal appeal.

In seeking to reach other men, the artist must rediscover the man in himself. He must establish a direct transmission of his inner feelings. This undefiled purity of exteriorization is the privilege of the great so-called primitive artists. With civilization the task of the artist has become more difficult. The original inspiration, before it reaches the spectator, is coated with layers of convention. Léger preserved his immediacy of perception, his directness of vision. In that sense he was a twentieth-century primitive. Many painters spend their lifetime rying to free themselves from the binding conventions; to wipe from their memory the obsessive, clinging academic teachings. Léger learned to forget, to be himself. Whatever struck his unprejudiced vision was worthy of striking the vision of others. He was his own testing ground. He knew that only in being true to himself does an artist have a chance of being true to others.

The way of reaching out of oneself, of communicating is, at first, mysteriously, by an inward path, as if the creative soul had to turn itself inside out before it could be free. This double movement, first inward before becoming outward, is the necessary safeguard of true art. An idea, a vision, needs to be tempered in the crucible of the creative soul. Only then will it acquire the immortal power to survive the corroding flow of time.

NOTES ON THE ILLUSTRATIONS

Fernand Léger. 1881–1955. Born, France.
Photographs taken in 1952, 1953, 1954.

85 *Still Life,* 1922. Oil, 25½″ × 19¾″. Collection Rupf, Bern.

86 Fernand Léger, photographed in 1952 in his Paris studio, wearing his favorite *casquette,* or workman's cap. Léger kept hanging in his studio the helmet that he wore in the First World War. He always referred to that world-shaking period as the turning point of his life and art.

87 Léger's palette, the only one in his Paris studio. After years of use, the paint was over three inches thick and looked like a relief map of mountains and craters.

88 Léger in his Paris studio, standing in front of his magnificent display wall. Hanging top left, *Le Grand Remorqueur,* 1923.

89 *Head,* 1952. Ink drawing. Private collection, New York.

90 A. The living room of his country house at Gif. On the wall, a portrait of Léger in wire by Calder.
B. The Gif studio. Léger liked to throw his sketches on the floor. On the far wall, his two contrasting styles: left, a version of *La Grande Parade* with the colors painted within the form; right, *La Partie de Campagne* with the color used independently.
C. Léger on the telephone.
D. His house at Gif, an abandoned inn which he bought and renovated a year before his death.
E. Léger was the only painter I saw who had a television set. On it, Russian *baba* toys; on the wall, a Léger ceramic.
F. Léger relaxing in a deck chair in his Gif studio. Behind him, a large black and white decoration in tile. At the bottom left, a portrait done when he was very young. Léger was seldom without it, as if it were a fetish.

91 *La Grande Parade,* the final version of Léger's last great masterpiece. H
made an extraordinary number of preliminary sketches in black and whit
and in color, then a great many smaller versions in oil, always seeking a solu
tion that would satisfy him. Finally, after great aesthetic conflict, he decide
to free color from line. He stands, solidly planted, a ragged, gay, earthy par
of the visual parade behind him.

VILLON

"What is inspiration? It is essentially a love of life that makes me conscious of th
air I breathe. I am hooked by life as by a woman." The man speaking, Jacque
Villon, is now eighty-five. His thin white hair seems blond; his cheeks are pin
and smooth. A slight build and an ease of movement contribute to him an aspec
of youth. The illusion is emphasized by an open shirt and soft sweater, slacks, ten
nis socks, and sandals.

His is an ageless face. Centuries of culture, of intellectual refinement, o
breeding can be traced in the subtle proportions of his features and bone struc
ture, the thin lips, the long nose, the high and rounded forehead. I thought of
scholar finely drawn by Holbein or a portrait of some nobleman by Clouet.

On his cheek appear two small warts. How often such accidents have had
tactile fascination for portrait painters, especially those of the Renaissance, an
how often such "defects" graft themselves on one's memory whereas perfec
smooth, monotonous form is soon forgotten.

In the presence of Villon one is inescapably conscious of France—*la douc
France,* gentle and charming. The very name Villon conjures up the image o
François Villon, the great ribald and tender poet of the fifteenth century.

The French intellectual is seldom a dry non-sensual man. To Jacques Villon
the abstract artist, nature is woman. "I am not tempted to philosophize abou
nature. I'd rather possess her," he said. Villon speaks of his art and his relation
with nature as a man of his mistress—a healthy desire to possess, uncomplicated b
complexes.

Since 1906, for more than half a century, Jacques Villon has lived in th
same studio in Puteaux, a Paris suburb, built on a hill that slopes gently dow
to the Seine. (Continuity of surroundings seems to have played an important rol
in many creative lives.) His studio, off a quiet provincial street that seems ver
far from Paris, is part of what was once an extraordinary community—the "Schoo
of Puteaux," of which Villon is now the only living master. One cannot get t
Villon's house without passing an old suburban villa once occupied by Frank
Kupka, one of the pioneers of abstract art. Villon's studio is a sad gray stucc
pavilion. Farther down in the shaded garden stands another building wher
Villon's brother, Raymond Duchamp-Villon, lived.

Kupka is dead. Villon is eighty-five. Recognition came slowly to these artists
and they symbolically stood aloof, as Cézanne in Aix, from the Paris where fo
so long they were not appreciated. There is no view from Villon's studio. Instea
there is the quiet sadness of a garden overgrown with grass and unweeded paths
All the houses on this street seem to exist on borrowed time; the city is encroach

ng, and soon they will be torn down and replaced by apartment houses that will se up this wasted space where a few sensitive creative men found their haven.

Villon is a Nordic, born in Rouen, Normandy—that extraordinary nursery f such great French artists as Poussin, Courbet, Léger, Dufy, and Braque. The ich northern province with its fields and seashore has for centuries mothered nd inspired artists. One must hear the pride with which Léger or Villon says, "I m Norman," implying in that short phrase heraldic deeds and peasant humble- ess—the spirit of the sailor and the shrewd cunning of a poacher. To be a Nor- man implies the ability to act and to execute, to put one's ideas into practical orm, to change with one's own hands dreams into concrete reality.

But above all there is the light of Normandy, that magic medium that trans- orms nature into an eye-stimulating color impulse. The haze from the North Sea eveals all the hues that the harsh sun of the south bleaches. The great schools of olorists have flourished near areas of water—the Venetians, the Dutch, the nglish, the impressionists near their rivers and seas, and then the Normans of ontemporary art.

"I was born in 1875. My mother was a Norman. She used to draw when she aw me paint as a child. My grandfather Émile Nicolle was an artist, an etcher who also sold marine insurance. I studied law, but at eighteen I failed in my xams."

Recalling life in Rouen, Villon said, "An artists' supply shop there had draw- ngs by Lautrec and Steinlen. A friend of mine wrote news articles about painters. n eighty-three-year-old aunt, or cousin, contributed notices on art to the news- apers and magazines of Rouen. She even wrote a play, and at a time when Rodin was hated she defended his art and him. There was a current of modernism, a tirring. . . .

"It made me want to leave Rouen and go toward the modern movement. I wanted fresh air. I went to Paris, to Montmartre. There I was surrounded by the avant-garde—no pompiers. I was a petit révolté." He added, "That was 1894. I adopted a pseudonym, Villon; our real name was Duchamp." He paused a mo- ment and said, "You see my father was a fine man. He was a notary; I was a révolté, but I did not want to hurt him. Now that I am successful, I am sorry to have changed my family name. How my conscience troubles me because of him!" As he spoke the stream of recollection brought animation to his gestures; his lips moved quickly in staccato, each word precisely formed. There was warmth, ten- derness, and an exceptional humanity in what he said—the words of a man who knew what family love meant.

"We've always been a tightly knit family. I was particularly close to my mid- dle brother, Duchamp-Villon. He had studied medicine, but during an illness he tried sculpting and became a sculptor. He lived in a studio next to mine for twelve years, until his death in 1918. At that time our younger brother, Marcel Duchamp, the painter, was always nearby. Marcel made a point of honor of being brighter and stronger than we were." Villon's eyes twinkled. "We taught Marcel to play chess; he learned so well that I could never beat him. We tried billiards; we used to play in a place called La Poule au Gibier. He beat us at that, too. I like games, but not money games. I don't gamble."

It is rare in the history of art for three brothers to achieve greatness. Those of the Duchamp-Villon family have. Duchamp-Villon, an early cubist, was one of the great sculptors of modern art. Marcel Duchamp, the painter, has had a profound and lasting influence on contemporary art.

Villon remembered. "Marcel went into abstract art because he could not stand all those people who raved about 'beautiful sunsets.'

"Marcel classified everything, even chance," Villon said. Duchamp's obsession with chance, his sense of irony, made him his own victim. He abandoned painting for chess, finding in the limitless speculation of mathematical laws of probability the answers to his hunger for speculation.

Although Duchamp gambled on the mysterious creativeness of accident, his older brother, Jacques Villon, believes that "one must avoid the accidental present. I want my art to be more general." In spite of their differences, these two have much in common: their sense of humor and, beyond it, irony, acute intelligence and love of scientific speculation. Villon is the classicist who has repressed much in order to achieve modernism within tradition. Duchamp is the romantic who broke with tradition, and too late realized that he had destroyed what he loved.

Villon then talked about himself. "In the early days, to earn a living, I illustrated newspapers. I would draw all night; it was a way of making money, and then most of my friends were doing it. A painter must have difficulties to surmount." His index finger pointed in emphasis. "But I won't say anything bad about newspapers! Journalism has not harmed literature. For an artist to illustrate newspapers is a contact with reality. He comes to grips with life. But when I think back on the fifteen years I worked for newspapers—in a way they were wasted. I could have painted that much longer.

"You see, my father had six children. He could send me only a little money and I wanted to make more. I should have contented myself with what he sent me and painted instead of wasting so much time. It was all a matter of pride—my desire to prove to my parents that I could manage on my own. If only I had been less proud." Apologetically he added, "I could have done so much better, but luckily, because of my long life, time has been given back to me.

"After I started painting I was always in a hurry. When I was on vacation, I tried to get back a week earlier. I had the feeling that I had to recapture the time lost. There is so little left to live. If I had died twenty years ago, there would not have been a painter Villon."

In the peace of his later life, in the protection of his marriage, Villon works. He said, "My wife watches over my health." Madame Villon, to whom he has been married since 1904, is a frail elderly woman. She has large, warm brown eyes, contrasting with the sharp, pale, cool eyes of Villon. Whereas his features are pointed, hers are round. Her slippered feet made no noise on the wooden floor. In the gentleness of their relationship there is a serenity that provides a calm and ideal climate for creative work. Their voices were never raised. I was struck by the tranquillity of their life, the quietness of the studio. Here in the remote suburb with its tree-cast shadows, was the peace of surroundings and of mind that allow quiet meditation and the cutting of the visual world into facets of Villon's vision.

My first impression of his studio was of gray austerity. The cold north light carefully equalized by white cheesecloth seemed to transfix every object as though caught and suspended in a white crystal. Light there seemed to have a density of ts own. I thought of Vermeer's figures eternally preserved for posterity in their trunks of light-crystal. Light as an object seemed to exist all the more because of the white plaster walls, the dust-gray wood floor. On the dark end of the gray scale were the black wicker armchairs, the black-painted staircase that led to the second floor of the studio. Light seemed even more luminous against this monochromatic backdrop. There was not a single colored object to distract the spell. There were never two paintings visible at the same time; Villon always turned one against the wall if he wanted to show a second. In that sad, eye-resting room the lone vibrant canvas became an explosion of color, as though all passion, all effort were concentrated into that one intensely burning spot. The canvas was a prism breaking up the white light of the studio into the rainbow of the spectrum.

When, after long hours of meditation and work, Villon puts a painting back on one of the neatly built storage shelves, the studio seems momentarily plunged in darkness, as though the artist-scientist, after putting away his laboratory equipment, switched off the light. As I looked at the painting he was showing me, there seemed no immediate connection between it and its surroundings. There was no continuity, no obvious link between the pure bright colors, the geometric shapes, and the seemingly indifferent studio. On a high shelf, a few plaster sculptures by his brother Duchamp-Villon caught light and dust. Nothing seems more melancholy than abandoned bas-reliefs.

On a dark wood provincial chest, curiously out of place in the austere surroundings, were some small toys, painted naked dolls next to brown cows and white sheep, all intermingled as though abandoned by a careless child. Like Poussin, the severe classicist who re-created his compositions in miniature theaters, studying light on draped terra-cotta figures, Villon works out his compositions with these toys. The accidental reality is eliminated, and the artist can work in the peace and security of his studio on the involved problems of composition and execution that art requires. "Art is a translation of nature that has more grandeur," he said.

On a table were several toy models of airplanes. With them this artist-scientist was experimenting, as the aeronautical engineer who tests his theories on miniature plane models in a wind tunnel. But here the more sensitive instruments—the human eye and brain—were testing in the wind tunnel of light that is Villon's studio. Here where objects could be manipulated, seen, and analyzed from all sides in a flow of vision, the artist could discover secrets that simple sketching from actual reality would never disclose. The crude simplification of these objects reduced them to rough essences of the things they represented. The airplanes and other toys were stand-ins for generalizations—human, animal, machine. Villon assigned to each its place in a seemingly new nature, not the one of everyday surroundings, but the one behind superficial appearances, the essential nature where the hidden structure of the universe is revealed.

One by one he picked up the toys and haphazardly placed them on a chessboard; it seemed as though the mathematical laws that govern chess suddenly governed these playful symbols. Villon with his toys and his chessboard was re-creating life in microcosm and, as in his art, rendering perceivable that which is too vast for us to perceive. As an artist who is also a man of science, he continues the tradition of the Renaissance. Leonardo da Vinci could well have been his master. The sketches of airplanes by Villon reminded me of the notebooks of Leonardo, where the first flying machines were prefigured.

On a small drawing table next to his canvas were several torn sheets of tracing paper—his palettes. On them he can mix his colors without one color's intruding on the other; the pure mixtures thus isolated permit methodical, precise work.

"I work with pure colors . . . straight from the tube. I don't add oil or turpentine. I don't worry what will happen. I am working only for the present!"

The bright canvas on the easel seemed to obey some hidden law of color harmony. Villon, the great colorist, explained. "My purpose is to reduce all colors to a unity, to give each color the same value, and to fill the gulf between them with white or maybe even black." From the large table littered with drawings he picked up a small book lovingly covered with neatly folded brown paper. It was the French edition of O. N. Rood's *Modern Chromatics,* published in 1881 in New York. "My system of the use of color is based on the study of this American scientist. I want to achieve harmony between all colors. The master craftsmen who worked with stained glass always took into consideration a unifying theory of colors." Rood in his book compares the luminosity of colors to white paper, and if white equals one hundred, each color will have its relative number.

Villon said, "Colors have different vibrations. If white, considered as a base, stands for one hundred, then yellow in relation to white will be eighty, vermilion twenty, ultramarine-blue seven, et cetera."

To achieve this harmony between all the colors in a painting, Villon has worked out his own rule of thumb. "I want to equalize the whole painting. To do that I must equalize all colors toward white. Suppose I have a yellow. To establish the quantity of white that I will add to it, I take the yellow, squeeze out some. With my palette knife I then divide my little mass of yellow in two equal parts. I say, I have fifty-fifty. I divide again—each one of the fifty parts into two, and twenty-five-twenty-five. Now I have to add white. I have to add nearly seventy-five, or three parts of white equal in size to the twenty-five quantity of yellow, in order to get seventy-five plus twenty-five equals one hundred. If I have a blue, which stands for seven, I have to add about ninety, or nine times the amount of blue in white paint.

"There need be no relationship between the sizes of white added to the yellow or the blue. The small quantity of white I added to the yellow is sufficient to give the yellow an equal value with the blue to which I had to add ninety. It is not complicated; I do it now instinctively." After many years Villon just squeezes his white tube, matching and measuring with the eye the correct amount of paint.

By this use of white in his colors, the white paint acting as a built-in light, Villon achieves a strange and personal color harmony. The colors of a Villon seem deceptively pale, as though bleached by an inner intense light, but this subtle gentle color sensation slowly grows more intense, insinuating, marking on the mind a permanent after-image. Whoever has looked at the sun and then closed his eyes knows the miraculous complementary color of the after-image, paler but so intense. A Villon painting is an after-image that one sees with open eyes.

Villon continued. "If I have made a colored study for a painting—I do this sometimes—the colored study is made from the colors of reality. But I do not leave them just as they are. I influence them. I intensify the original sensation. The original sensation is altered, influenced by the colors I have chosen on the chromatic circle. After I have finished a painting, I sometimes rework it and influence the whole with a yellow, for example. It unifies the canvas. It is not a bad thing to do. There is a division in my work: color gives the sumptuousness, the richness of the opera; and the explaining is done by drawing.

"First, I make notations from nature; then I redo them, making a more complete drawing, stressing the main values. These main values I use as a base for the division of the subject into planes.

"There can be a rear plane, a middle plane, and a forward plane. There can be subdivisions of these planes, but, as much as possible, I limit myself to three planes. Each of these planes is colored, after I have chosen a scale on the chromatic circle. With three planes the chromatic harmony is usually of three colors. Each plane is influenced by one of the colors. For instance, if I am painting a face, the particular planes of the nose, the cheeks, et cetera, will be indicated in the color of their plane in general. I try to have, between the planes of color, neutral planes. These are the planes of rest. I express myself principally through planes."

Later Villon and I went into the living quarters. The small rooms contrasted with the gray but luminous vastness of the studio. Madame Villon was in the dining room, patiently reading a newspaper—the wife who knows what patience means, for to be the wife of a painter is to have the ability to wait. As she sat in the dark room, she seemed to blend with the surroundings, as though she were in an interior painted by Vuillard. Leafy shadows added a green dominant to the weak light that bathed the simple white wicker furniture. Near the window a table was set for a frugal lunch; these two would calmly break their bread together, undisturbed, and in this interlude the artist would find strength to resume where he left off. Nothing would jar him or tear the continuity of his creative thoughts. "I get up at eight in the morning and paint from nine till lunchtime," he told me. "After lunch, around three o'clock, I paint again. I take a two-week vacation every year."

Absorbing the austere surroundings, I realized that this was not a picture-making interior; this was the house of Monsieur and Madame Villon and it was apart from his art. It could not, in its neutral simplicity, interfere and intrude into his painting.

Villon is exceptionally articulate; his intelligence, the quickness, the precise analytical quality of his mind permit a revealing study of the artist. Through Villon one can grasp the thought behind the creative act of the modern artist.

"Painting is a form of the *élan vital,* the vital impulse," he said. "It is one of the forms of love. I am always attempting to join the two—love and painting—they are Siamese twins." He has found happiness in painting; but he said, "One suffers to produce it. It is not a happiness exposed in bright sunlight. It is a happiness that one must gain piece by piece. If a canvas 'rings,' if it is successful, then there is restitution." After a pause—"There is no immediate happiness," he added.

I asked him why he painted. "One has to pass one's time on the earth!" he answered, smiling his shy smile. "It is not necessary to paint. I don't believe in the modern artists' justifying their blobs of paint as instinctive. Only those who have studied have a right to modern expression. Probably the discipline, the moderation of my art comes from my bourgeois wisdom. Art for me is an opportunity to be happy. The tragedy of some painters is that they have an aspiration for beauty but don't attain it. We are not gods! Some painters look at themselves in a mirror and say, 'I am going to surpass my vision.' They cannot, and rage."

This French *bon sens,* which warns when to admit the impossible, is typical of Villon. His method of work, his life are a calm, serene flow; the wisdom of the French philosophers is in him.

"Art," he said, "is a distillation of emotional and physical origin in which intelligence wins over intuition."

During the First World War Villon worked as a cartographer for the army. Many painters bear the mysterious, lasting influence of some early craft: stained glass for Rouault, photo retouching for Chagall, architecture for Léger, house painting for Braque, perhaps map-making for Villon. He said, "I decompose the subject into planes and my painting is a working drawing by which to read reality." Then, too, there are the years Villon spent working on etchings. "Maybe the differences of bite of the acids made me realize strongly the differences of planes," he explained.

Whoever has seen military staff maps with cross-sections indicating the changes of level in the ridges, the hills, and the mountains knows the importance of variations of levels. The slopes and ridges, translated pictorially, show a world of surfaces and edges. The thin line of the edges in a Villon painting is the clash of two color surfaces, the frontier where their color maximums meet. Any line drawn on any surface gives a new meaning; it is a ridge of the imaginary levels that surround it, and all flatness seems to disappear from our perception as we become familiar with this notion. Then we see lines in paintings with new eyes.

The scientific study of vision undertaken during the Second World War to teach pilots safe landing methods has proved the importance of gradients (the gradient of a hill is its change of altitude with distance) and the importance of edges that cause changes of light energy, which in turn stimulate the eye.

As I write about these findings, a Villon painting comes to mind, its surfaces, edges, conflicts of light stimulation, those essential requirements for maximum perception. If Villon's art is difficult it is because it is so advanced. Twentieth century art is much less developed than twentieth-century science. But our understanding of new signs is rapidly increasing, and the seemingly incomprehensible but daring vision of the artist is a new facet of reality that the artist detects and reveals ahead of his time.

Villon finds geometry useful for the organization of his paintings. "I am constantly preoccupied with the pyramid of Da Vinci," he said. "We perceive things in a pyramidal way. Let's say the apex is in the eye and the base is in the object seen, or vice versa. As a matter of fact, both can coexist—a sort of going and coming between the eye and the object. This interpenetration of double pyramids gives movement to a painting and at the same time ties it together.

"Then if one draws the diagonals of a canvas, the intersection is the summit of four pyramids. The extremes of value will be, let's say, on the opposite sides of the pyramid. A painting has its own light not connected with the light of reality. The choice of what my painting is going to be is made before the execution begins. I do not like to repaint."

Villon paused, then said, "All these systems, I use them roughly, but their great advantage in creative work is that they force me to reflect. This way I do not start working at random.

"Study is very important, study should be used to make plans. I like to collect evidence for my paintings, to make studies from nature before I start working. Study is to me what scales are to a pianist. Little by little, I discover harmonies in my study, harmonies that are to be brought out so that the painting can have a personality that it owes to itself and to its source without being merely a copy.

"My paintings always have their origin in reality. I stir the source around in every direction, but I always need contact with the earth."

"What is the relationship between the artist and the outside world?" I asked. "Is there a correspondence that starts the creative act?"

"There is an appeal, a call," he answered. "One's mind recognizes certain forms. The subject is, perhaps, not very important. I became interested in airplanes because of their general rhythm. Rhythm has great importance. An airplane is in the air, it flies; one can see it as a whole, which is effective. I choose my drawings by their rhythm."

Villon went on. "I haven't a good visual memory; I remember poorly; I must lean on nature. I do not flee reality. In my most extreme paintings I like to hold on to reality."

More than any other modern artist, Villon has reconciled the two opposing movements of contemporary art—abstraction and realism. This synthesis may well be the solution to many of the dead ends of art.

Villon has been called the Cézanne of modern art. Like the classicists, Cézanne believed that great art must be based on a theory and a system and not rely on the accidental, intuitive handling of paint. "To re-create Poussin from nature" meant to Cézanne to superimpose on our vision of reality the laws of composition, geometry, the laws of number which since Plato have governed all great art. Cézanne, however, lived on the threshold of the twentieth century. The Scientific Age was to him a vision of the future. He felt that he was the "first marker on the new path; others will come." But Cézanne, perhaps, was too human and too passionate to realize fully the severe vision of his mind. It is as though Cézanne proceeded with intuitive logic, and Villon with scientific method. A man of thirty when Cézanne died, Villon has benefited fully from the great development of science. He is the painter-scientist who with infinite patience and discipline pursues his research.

He told me, "I have a difficulty in speaking about art. All that I have done all my life is search. When one seeks, one cannot put precisely into words what he has not yet found."

Never in any other artist's work have I seen a clearer manifestation of the sum of the mentally torturing, physically exhausting actions that go into the creation of a truly thought-out work of art. Yet Villon's art is not cold, for where Poussin, in his severe seventeenth-century French classicism, re-created the chilling, gray-shaded stillness of antique marble, Villon has used the vitalizing energy of pure color to express his severe compositions. He is fortunate to have inherited his intense palette from Seurat and the impressionists, but above all from such daring visual scientists as Chevreul.

When Villon sat down to paint, he picked up his brushes, and among them stuck out a ruler. With this restraint in hand he works. "There must be a discipline. One must sit down in front of the easel without waiting for inspiration. Inspiration has its place, but at a different moment. Inspiration in painting must be reduced rather than increased. If one increases it, one arrives at a false inspiration. Cennino Cennini orders artists to pray before they start working. That is so that they do not rush to their canvases and start putting down colors by accident. A preliminary meditation is necessary. It predisposes and forces one to concentrate and not to let oneself go at random.

"For a long time, I painted very freely," Villon said, "but I felt the need to meditate, reflect, organize. Now I submit to the laws of color and of the chromatic scale. This submission allows me to get ready; it is a preparation. Chance notation is good in a study, but after that one must bring order. Laws of color are not absolute, but important. Now I bring my work back to the laws of color —chromatic circle. I believe that the division of the canvas by the golden section helps a great deal.

"There is an inner discipline too that, in a way, controls everything. Even in the work of the abstractionists, where chance seems to dominate, there is a play of memory.

"I like to concentrate on a drawing without having other preoccupations and then to organize it into a painting. Above all, I am conscious of organization. I seek to avoid confusion. A work of art is more than just a conversation, it is a discourse. One must strengthen the thought behind a painting. Organization gives a rhythm on which drawing can lean. The drawing is not confined but rather held together by the laws of organization, and not governed simply by taste.

"Taste is a dangerous thing, especially for painting. After I have made a study drawing, I transform it by stressing rhythm. I avoid transforming because of taste, just to have it look good. If one paints just to record a bouquet of flowers, then taste is enough. But if one wants to magnify the bouquet of flowers, one must make a cathedral out of it, transform it. In art one must erect, one must go beyond the painting. My ambition is to explode the object and to make it, in exploding, reach the edges of the canvas, thus creating a new object."

Later he said, "Painting has changed and will change again, given new mechanical means of self-expression. The painting of today is a tributary of the painting of the past. I do not feel the need to redo *Sardanapale,* or the great subjects of the nineteenth-century painters. The painting of the future will not have to express all that we were obliged or wanted to express.

"In ten thousand years will there still be painting? Will there be a need to paint? One wonders if maybe art, beauty, and truth are not as absolute as one believes. I wonder if they are not relative, relative to the times, to manners, and customs. Yet there is something more than taste."

On a large worktable in his studio were many sketchbooks and loose sheets of drawing paper. He said, "When I was young I made many sketches, now very few, but I have found that when I now feel the necessity to sketch there is a real significance."

This statement revealed a curious ability of his mind to take with a grain of salt whatever happened to him. Certain sentences reveal graphically the structure of the inner mental processes and permit the intimate study of a man's mind.

Villon is *un homme d'esprit*. In the French language the one word *esprit* stands for humor but also soul, mind, sense, understanding, intellect, wit, fancy, temper, character. The dignity of man is his mind. Intelligence is the weapon he uses in his struggle with the universe; with it, man is slowly unlocking the many closed doors that bar progress toward understanding. The mystic, the philosopher, the scientist, the artist are but names given to men of the mind, who seek in their own chosen ways the answers to their questions. Their search for the truth is a measure of man's faith.

When I watched Villon work and live, listened to Villon speak, the great aged artist seemed to be "the portrait of the artist as a young man." It seemed as if James Joyce had prefigured Villon's existence and thoughts—as if the painter ahead of his time confirmed the vision of the writer who wrote of art: "To speak of . . . things and to try to understand their nature, and having understood it, to try slowly and humbly and constantly to express, to press out again, from the gross earth or what it brings forth, from sound and shape and color, which are the prison gates of our soul, an image of the beauty we have come to understand— that is art."

NOTES ON THE ILLUSTRATIONS

Jacques Villon (Gaston Duchamp). 1875–1963. Born, France.
Photographs taken in 1950, 1954, 1957, 1959.

92 Jacques Villon at seventy-nine. The model of an airplane in his hand expresses his vision of space.

93 The interior of Villon's Puteaux studio. His easel nearly always stands in front of the same wall. Through the years very little changes in the things surrounding him; only the new paintings reflect the changes in the vision of the artist. The two canvases are in his great late manner (1958). The sculptures are all the work of his brother Raymond Duchamp-Villon, one of the great sculptors of the cubist generation. On the floor, Villon's gouache studies.

94 Villon meditating on an unfinished work based on a study of airplanes in space. He sat in his favorite rocking chair.

95 Villon's hand squeezing out white, the paint that is the artist's light. It is added in measured amounts to all colors, bringing them into luminous balance. He uses paper palettes because they can be thrown away, but now his admirers collect them.

96 The Villons in their dining room—a moment of quiet, rest in the small, dark room behind the large, light studio. Madame Villon (Gaby) is reading.

97 A. Lying on a chessboard, models of airplanes and Villon's color wheel, on which he works out his color theories.

B. On another table, preparatory realistic sketches for a book he was illustrating. They are the first elements in his work process; from them he will create the final abstracted vision.

C. In his living room, a family souvenir from Rouen.

D. The toys that he uses to work out his compositions.

E. The wooden mannequins for the study of movement.

F. Villon's hand playfully arranging a composition.

G. On the mantelpiece in the living room, Oriental sculpture.

H. An exterior view of the Puteaux studio.

I. The meal of the artist.

J. The skylight of his studio, a pure pattern of geometric lines.

K. A plaster of *The Cock*, by his brother Duchamp-Villon. Telephone numbers have been irreverently jotted on it.

L. Madame Villon on the telephone.

DUCHAMP

His face tortured with subtleties, his hands moving in a courtly ballet, Marcel Duchamp has a strange, regal presence, an ecclesiastical authority. Only the prelate's robes are missing. He is a truly Renaissance man, a curious mixture of poetry, earthiness, and cunning. In his New York apartment are many sets of chess, the game with which he is obsessed, perhaps because in it he finds a sublimation for power. Duchamp is a professional chess-player. "I never abandoned painting for chess," he said. "That is a legend. It is always that way. Just because a man starts to paint does not mean he has to go on painting. He isn't even obliged to abandon it. He just doesn't do it any more, just as one doesn't make omelets if he prefers meat. I do not see the need to classify people, and, above all, to treat painting as a profession. I don't see why people try to make civil servants out of painters, officials of the Ministry of Fine Arts. There are those who obtain medals and those who make paintings."

Duchamp is the aristocrat of modern art. He has the haughtiness that comes with the dismissal of creative torment. He has put an end to his creative suffering; but even before this his hands did not have to be sullied for him to create. He had the arrogant vision to see and to confer art upon what he deigned to see.

Marcel Duchamp, the man who painted a mustache on the Mona Lisa to show his contempt and irreverence for the sacrosanct attitudes that he felt were stifling the creativeness of young artists, shocked America with his *Nude Descending a Staircase,* in the 1913 New York Armory Show. He was one of the first dadaists, the group which started out in 1916 as a revolt against traditional art. His was a revolt against academic aesthetics; he wanted art without art. Marcel Duchamp was one of the first to discover the "ready-made"; he realized that the everyday object could be transformed by artistic selection into an object with aesthetic qualities.

During our conversation he said, "There are too many artists. When there are so many artists, all possible, all good, then nothing is good. In each century there are no more than one or two geniuses. Otherwise art becomes a profession, a handicraft, and a painter makes a good painting just as a cabinetmaker makes a good piece of furniture.

"Today the artist is free, free to die of hunger. An artist should have no social obligations. If he marries, has children, he very soon becomes a victim. He must earn money to feed his family. Only one person who does not have to be fed is easier than three or four. To increase the number of people around an artist is a calamity. By forty or fifty he can earn his living comfortably, but thirty years have gone by during which he had to compromise to do it. An artist must be an egotist. He must be completely blind to other human beings—egocentric in the grand manner. It is unavoidable, one cannot create great things if he is only half involved and in doubt. The life of an artist is like the life of a monk, a lewd monk if you like, very Rabelaisian. It is an ordination."

NOTES ON THE ILLUSTRATIONS

Marcel Duchamp. 1887–. Born, France.
Photographs taken in 1959.

98 Marcel Duchamp's hands as he plays chess.

99 Duchamp, in the living room of his New York apartment, standing before his work on glass, *Neuf Moules Mâlic*, 1914–1915. This is a study for his great *La Mariée Mise a Nu par ses Célibataires*.

PEVSNER

Antoine Pevsner and his brother Nahum Gabo are Russian-born pioneers of twentieth-century sculpture. The originators of constructivism, they discovered a new use for metals and welding and made a new marriage of art and mathematics. Pevsner's studio on the outskirts of Paris is filled with carefully displayed sculptures, each one breaking up space in a willfully preconceived manner. When I visited him there he was wearing a deep pink shirt and a matching tie. The lenses of his thick horn-rimmed glasses were orange. Dressed in his romantic colors, this gentle man seemed surprised by the sculptured materializations, the shapes of his ideas. These sculptures are the movements of his brain made visible by firing. With his blowtorch and oxygen mask he withdraws, like a new Vulcan, into his working area. An artist ahead of his time, Pevsner uses as artistic tools the precision instruments of an engineer. "Art must be inspiration controlled by mathematics," he said. "I have a need for peace, symphony, orchestration."

NOTES ON THE ILLUSTRATIONS

Antoine Pevsner. 1886–1962. Born, Russia.
Photographs taken in 1953.

100 Pevsner in his studio and, in the foreground, his *Projection dynamique au 30e degré*, 1950–1951.

101 One of the first to use the blowtorch in sculpture, Pevsner is here putting the finishing touches on *Construction Cinétique,* 1953. The rare surface texture is achieved by welding copper rods onto a basic sculptural form.

ARP

Jean Arp is one of the giants of modern art. His share in the shaping of the new image of the world around us is, and has been for a long time, dominant. One of the founders of dadaism as far back as 1916, he pursues his iconoclastic creation with a serenity that only supreme self-confidence can give. After years of being left in relative peace, now that the abstract century has begun he emerges as the shape-maker of things present and to come.

When I last saw him, he stood in the long narrow studio as if hemmed in by the inventiveness of his all-white perfect forms. He remained motionless, deep in thought; then, an unexpected gesture of his hands, a movement of expression across his face made me sense that behind his deceptive scholarly calm lurked a wit destructive yet essentially kind. A quick, shy smile broke the Olympian mask to reveal for an instant that the most serious creative act can have its roots in humor and in a sense of play. The source of his adventure is perhaps the release that laughter gives to inspiration.

NOTES ON THE ILLUSTRATIONS

Jean Arp. 1887–1966. Born, Alsace.
Photographs taken in 1959.

102 His sculpture studio is at one end of Arp's garden, and in the house itself Arp has this second studio-living-room. The large worktable is strewn with drawings and paper, wood, and metal cutouts. On the walls hang wooden reliefs. All around the room, plasters for bronzes. Above this room Arp has a private study hung with the works of his first wife, one of the great abstract artists, Sophie Taeuber-Arp. (He remarried in 1959.) These two great artists sometimes worked together at the same creation. Arp showed me a collage they did. He said, "We attempted perfection; we wanted an object to be without flaw, so we cut the papers with a razor, pasted them down meticulously, but it buckled and was ruined . . . that is why we decided to tear prewrinkled paper, so that in the finished work of art imperfection would be an integral part, as if at birth death were built in."

103 Jean Arp in a playful moment in his sculpture studio. He is surrounded by his plaster casts.

LÉGER 87

89

LÉGER

90

A B

C D

E F

92   VILLON

VILLON

VILLON 97

E F

G H

I J
K L

DUCHAMP

100

PEVSNER

ARP

IV
FIVE PAINTERS IN PARIS

UTRILLO   SEGONZAC   GROMAIRE   LAURENCIN   BORÈS

UTRILLO

Under the Second Empire, when it was fashionable to live on the outskirts of Paris, the rich new society of Napoleon III built large villas in the suburbs of Chatou and Le Vésinet. Today these estates with their parks and gardens have been broken up into small lots, with one- or two-story houses that bear such pathetic names as "Çamsuffit," or "Good enough for me." This suburb, where Maurice Utrillo lived, is sadder than the poorest workers' districts. Its avenues are bricked in by walls. One rings several times before being admitted through the forbidding iron doors barring these houses from the outside world.

I visited Utrillo in 1949. From the outside, his villa, with its high walls of gray cement, was indistinguishable from its equally drab neighbors. But after ringing at the gate, I was somewhat surprised to have the door opened by a butler-gardener in a blue apron. At the end of a meticulously cropped lawn dotted with pseudoclassical statues, bird cages, and pergolas, stood a gay pink villa with orange sunshades, a house one would expect to see only under the bright Mediterranean sun.

Madame Utrillo, who is also an artist and paints under the name of Lucie Vallore, came out of the villa. She is short and stocky, with a square peasant face. She wears no make-up; her mouth is wide and mobile. She talked incessantly.

Madame reclined in a deck chair in the shade of a pergola and spoke of ambassadors, authors, princes, and Hollywood stars. "We were invited to go to the wedding of Rita Hayworth," she said. "Rita is a great friend. I ordered my husband a blue suit so that he would look more like a master." She spoke mostly about herself, Lucie Vallore, the painter. It was difficult to find out about Maurice Utrillo. She gave the impression of a monologist occupying the stage because the principal had been delayed or unable to perform.

After interminable chatter we walked toward the house. The red-orange shades were half drawn over the large glass doors of the dining room. Suddenly a ravaged face appeared from behind the glass, an elongated face with deep furrows and large dark pockets under downcast eyes. The face remained immobile for a few instants, its glance averted, all the more tragic in its gay frame of sunlit pink walls and orange shades. It remained motionless, as if waiting for an incentive to move. The gardener-butler rushed up to open the door. A tall, stooped man with a thin streak of gray hair over his balding forehead shuffled slowly into the glare of the sunlight.

Utrillo wore blue painter's trousers, an Eisenhower jacket, a shirt with a stud but no tie; his feet were clad in the familiar checked-felt slippers of French concierges. His wife seemed to have dressed him for the occasion, but his clothes were too small for him. The sleeves of his shirt hung limply over his small, lean hands. His thumbs were folded inside his clenched fists.

An academic statue of a classically draped woman holding a palette in her hand stood in the garden. This Muse of Painting, probably left over from some imposing Beaux-Arts monument, was surrounded by rows of little red begonias and a minuscule, toylike green fence. Utrillo looked at the goddess of his household as though he were seeing it for the first time. He shuffled toward the statue, examined it with curiosity and surprise, shuffled away, bewildered. Madame Utrillo followed behind her husband and turned him in whatever direction she saw fit, saying, as to a child, "Answer the gentleman, turn and smile; the gentleman wants to take your picture." He responded with monosyllabic sounds.

A haunting tragedy was painted on Utrillo's physical self. The ever-averted eyes, the downcast face, the drooping sadness of his frame cried out for help. This man gave the impression that he did not enjoy life and wanted no part of it, that he had relinquished any control. One did not even feel his presence in his own home. Madame dominated the household.

The villa was overcrowded with fantastic baroque furniture—huge eighteenth-century side tables, consoles, chandeliers, grand pianos covered with inscribed photographs of celebrities. Hanging on the walls of the main living room were small Utrillos, the typical scenes of Paris that he had painted all his life.

The adjoining room, a library, was like a small oasis of filial love. Here there were no Utrillos, only paintings and drawings by his mother, Suzanne Valadon. Neither were there any of his paintings in his own bedroom, a boudoir-like room decorated in an exclusively feminine, rich, and contemporary manner, all crystal and satin. The walls were adorned with Madame Utrillo's paintings.

Madame walked around her husband, asking, "Darling, don't you think I'm talented? Don't you like my work? Tell the man," she prodded, "what you think of my work. Don't you think I have made progress?" Utrillo emerged from his dreamlike silence to answer, "Yes, yes, oh yes." He bought his peace, his right to live his way by agreeing. But she wanted more than obedience; she needed approval and asked for proofs of love. These manifestations are scattered all over the house. On a palette that he gave her as a wedding-anniversary present he had inscribed, "To my good darling Lucie, her Maurice Utrillo—Thursday, 25th of August, 1938."

His own studio, at the end of a narrow black corridor, was a very small room, about eight by ten feet, with a tiny window. It could have been a maid's room. A small easel held a canvas on which he was working—the familiar houses, a *moulin*. Human beings, more important than in his early work, were represented in naïve, childish bottle shapes. Next to the easel was a collection of postcards, one of his great sources of inspiration. A small decorator's table supported his palette. This palette was revealing. On its rectangular wooden surface rose a high pile of white pigment. Four or five colors were neatly aligned at one corner in small dabs. There were a rag, many palette knives—and brushes; one suddenly understood that this was not just a painter's palette: to this man who had spent his life painting walls, houses, and churches made of stone and plaster, the palette was a plasterer's trowel. The mass of white was not just paint pigment but plaster and cement that he applied like a mason to his canvas.

What is the mysterious power of Utrillo's art? Why do his seemingly naïve landscapes haunt the onlooker? Unlike the true primitive who straightforwardly states his spontaneous vision, Utrillo hid under a guise of innocence his real tragedy and suffering. This ability to combine charm and ugliness, to coat suffering with the illusion of serenity creates the poetic sensation particular to his art. The impersonality of his scenes, the severe discipline that architecture (his favorite theme) imposed on his emotions, brought his art to the brink of greatness, to the classic universality of the artist who has dominated his ego.

"For the Greatest the Fool is the pencil more Blest
And when they are drunk they always paint best."
—William Blake

Utrillo was an alcoholic. One might have expected from him an expressionistic, tormented vision, but his best paintings have the solidity of stone. Where Cézanne sensed that one had to discover structure in the universe, Utrillo, with the simpler approach of a less intellectual artist, groped for structure and found it in his subject matter—buildings. This search for structure and solidity as a refuge for a reeling mind led him toward great art. His suffering and striving, his struggle with himself, also led Utrillo to God.

The dangerous quietness of Utrillo's manner, and the curious twisted smile that occasionally pierced his face reminded me of Rouault, another painter-mystic. Religion is both in the background and on the surface of Rouault's art. In Utrillo it is a more subconscious layer that has exposed itself in his obsession for painting churches. Rouault, who seldom painted architecture, expressed religion through the human form. Utrillo, who always avoided the direct portrayal of the human form, expressed his religion in the buildings of faith. One was preoccupied with the human aspects of faith, the other with the stones of churches. But the distorted faces of Rouault and the leprous walls of Utrillo's houses are both aspects of the human tragedy.

An ordinary chest of dark wood in Utrillo's studio held a large collection of religious objects. There was no aesthetic choice in their selection; they belonged to the sentimental nineteenth-century religious art of Saint-Sulpice. They were objects of faith on its simplest level: yellow plaster statuettes of St. Vincent and St. Theresa, a statue of Utrillo's patron saint, Joan of Arc, holding her sword in a rapture of prayer. Behind this chromo art stood some graver objects of faith, a few black medieval crucifixes, as though a deeper mysticism buttressed Utrillo's everyday religion. The window of the studio opened on a small gray cement building with geraniums in front of the door. This was his private chapel, where he spent many hours of his day in prayer.

In the humility of Utrillo's art, the innocence of his vision, the humbleness of his subject matter, the modesty of his aesthetic approach, he is never the artist rivaling or substituting himself for the Creator. He touches the spectator and brings out sympathy and love. This is the painted suffering of a sinner seeking redemption. Utrillo was hurt by the cruelty of the human race, which too often finds pleasure in tormenting the sick and the feeble. He found shelter from its laughs and pranks in the shuttered houses that he painted. And the love that he had to express and could not give to humanity he gave to God's nature.

NOTES ON THE ILLUSTRATIONS

Maurice Utrillo. 1883–1955. Born, France.
Photographs taken in 1949.

104 *The Little Church,* 1912. Oil, 26¾" × 20⅞". Private collection, Geneva.

105 Maurice Utrillo with his wife, the painter Lucie Vallore, in the garden of their house in the Vésinet—Utrillo absent, lost in his dream. His wife was to him nurse, manager, and loving tyrant. The house, La Bonne Lucie, is named after her.

SEGONZAC

When I drove to visit Segonzac near Versailles, the road to his house was partially blocked for repairs. So that I would not have any inconvenience in finding his house, he had asked a friend to meet me a kilometer ahead of the roadblock. This subtle politeness and consideration are typical of Segonzac, an extraordinarily charming, elegant, worldly, intelligent man. As I looked at his strong Gascon nose, his dashing clipped mustache, his casual, elegant attire, I thought of an intelligent D'Artagnan, full of dash and physical prowess. No wonder boxers, fencers, cyclists, in fact the entire world of sport, fascinate this *seigneur*. His manner of walking with the torso leaning somewhat forward, hips stiff and legs alternately thrown forward, feet slightly turned out, made me think of an elderly courtier walking through the hall of mirrors in the golden days of Versailles. Here is the artist *gentilhomme*. André Dunoyer de Segonzac is the only nobleman of all the great French painters alive today.

In his small beautifully proportioned villa near Paris I felt as though I were visiting a small château. The living room, attractively furnished with Provençal furniture, gives a sense of comfort and enjoyment. This is a true living room, with sofas, armchairs, bookcases and tables, flowers everywhere, lace curtains. A plaster cast of a Venus standing in a corner on a sculptor's stand is the only quick signal that art is on the mind of the owner. Hanging unobtrusively on the walls are ink drawings of landscapes; they are there for you to find. The tall bookcase is full of magnificent books illustrated by Segonzac, but I had to open the bookcase, and open the books, to find Segonzac's art. Nowhere in this painter's house is art obviously present on first impression.

Segonzac's studio is a part of the whole house. It differs very little from the other rooms; the windows are slightly larger. On the walls are several paintings by friends—no one famous, just paintings that Segonzac likes. The furniture, light wood Louis Philippe armchairs and chest of drawers, is as attractive as that in the living room. Here, of course, there are some humbler objects, dishes, plates, jars, a parasol, plaster cast, some lemons, and a green garden table—objects which figure in many of his paintings.

The deep corner of the studio has in it one of the largest canvases that Segonzac painted, a Rembrandt-like study of two workers drinking in a cabaret. Segonzac said, "Notice the date." It is 1907, just after Cézanne's death, and about the time cubism was born; yet this naturalistic dark brown monochromatic study of two drinkers shows only a deep desire to convey a mood. Segonzac's work is closer to Rembrandt's than to the French master's. Segonzac has never deviated through all the tempestuous years of modern art, braving the passing experiments with an aristocratic self-assurance. Sure of himself and confident of his vision, Segonzac has been able to navigate serenely through life, pursuing only one course, while other painters of his generation have experimented at one time or another with fauvism, cubism, impressionism, or other styles. If he has experimented at all, it is only with texture and medium better to achieve his end, the rendition of nature. Segonzac's inspiration is nature, and his paintings are done from the motif itself. For outdoor painting Segonzac has designed an immense palette that he can put on his knees. I have never seen another palette like this. It is about four to five feet high, the inside edge of the longer side curved so that the body of the artist can fit into it. With this palette on his knees, Segonzac is literally sitting amid his color.

The theme of his illustrations for the *Géorgiques* is the vineyards of southern France. The work and the movement of the laborers in the field are the themes for many of his finest paintings and drawings. Segonzac understands and paints the French countryside with precise knowledge. His water colors of small villages are some of the most moving portrayals of the French scene.

As we relaxed and drank wine from beautiful deep green, peasantlike bottles —white, greenish, yellow dry wine—Segonzac spoke easily and precisely with a worldliness that permitted communication. There was no showing off, only a friendly desire to appear in a pleasing aspect and a self-consciousness of how he would be portrayed. When I showed him some photographs I had taken of other artists, more or less unconscious of being photographed, he felt as though he had posed perhaps too much, that he had been slightly unnatural.

He is a rare example of that French phenomenon, culture without intellectuality. His erudition and his knowledge are part of his whole formative process. Art, literature, music are as necessary to him as any other manifestations of nature. They are all taken as such and not as escapes into a metaphysical or theological world; in fact, he has contempt for the intellectual abracadabra of modern thinking in which so many artists have been trapped.

The answer to everything for Segonzac is in nature. It is in communion with nature that man finds himself. Segonzac goes alone into the countryside with his canvas or sketchbook, surrounded by his colors, surrounded by his element, nature, and creates. The simple, direct clarity of his creative process and of his life is refreshing. The sun-surrounded interiors, the well-kept house with its beautiful furniture, flowers, and paintings, and, above all, Segonzac, the elegant, worldly host, are rare in the world of modern art, which seems to be surrounded by anguish and suffering as if of necessity.

André Dunoyer de Segonzac. 1884–. Born, France.
Photographs taken in 1953.

106 *Entrance to the Ménagerie, Versailles,* 1925. Etching. The Museum of Modern Art, New York.

107 Segonzac on the terrace of his house near Paris. The fantastic palette is his own invention. When he sits down to paint, it allows him to be surrounded by his colors.

GROMAIRE

The rich dark ochers and browns of Marcel Gromaire's paintings contrast strikingly with the dark wood of the furniture and of the African sculptures in his Paris studio, one vast room in a modern private house. The sensuousness of the elaborately carved chests, glowing with the patina of time, is repeated in Gromaire's caressingly painted forms. Stacked in neat piles on a dark wood table and pinned in neat rows on straw-colored walls are dozens of drawings in black and white, their scratchy lines of ink filigrees cast over luminous squares of white paper. The studio seems dark, and only sharp accents of strong light bounce against the eye. Through this ordered wealth of textural sensation Gromaire gradually interprets and transposes reality onto his canvas. When a painting he is working on finally fits into the private universe of his studio, it is truly finished. Gromaire uses his studio as a standard, a filter; it is more than just a place to paint.

At sixty-eight, Gromaire is a blond pink-cheeked giant, secure in his vision of life and art. His concept of the rules of art is strict; he has the kind of restraint from which real freedom is born. "The thing that dominates everything else in the plastic arts is form," he said. "Now form is rejected, and particularly human form. There are very few who through the centuries have discovered living forms. Creation does not mean anything. The great method for man in art or science is the experimental method. All the progress of humanity has been achieved through experiment, and not through pseudo-invention. Nothing is invented. One only thinks he invents in order to give himself license. I am against the *a priori* rejection of things that are constants. We live among human beings, we have a form. Why reject all this for phantom forms that do not, in most instances, correspond to a deep reality? Abstraction only takes on real value when it comes into contact with concrete reality. It is the fusion of the two that makes the explosion. Left to itself, abstraction liquefies, becomes decorative."

NOTES ON THE ILLUSTRATIONS

Marcel Gromaire. 1892–. Born, France.
Photographs taken in 1952.

108 Gromaire's pen-and-ink studies pinned neatly on the wall.

109 Marcel Gromaire at work in his Paris studio on a bold stylization of nature, a painting of trees.

LAURENCIN

Revolt takes on various guises; the brutal or severe are not the only aspects of courage. When Marie Laurencin painted her tender visions, she attempted to reaffirm feminine seduction in the face of the victorious modernism. The femininity of her art is the inevitable complement to the arrogant masculinity of cubism.

Only an easel and a few painter's tools intruded on the attractive serenity of her Paris salon. A mandolin with ribbons and flowers hung on a wall. Three accents of white—her hair gently pulled back, a long rope of pearls, a jabot at her throat—accentuated the severity of her black dress. Her tender, pale eyes and the gentle, mannered movements of her sensitive lips softened the image of propriety. Her gestures were calm, her voice low. To preserve the past she pursued the ritual of graceful existence. Through the daily practice of her pastel-hued art, she achieved a link with poetry.

NOTES ON THE ILLUSTRATIONS

Marie Laurencin. 1885–1956. Born, France.
Photographs taken in 1949.

110 Marie Laurencin reflected in the mirrors of her Paris house.

111 *Tillya,* 1925. Oil, 18⅛″ × 15″.

BORÈS

Francisco Borès lives with his Russian wife and two children in a fifth-floor walk-up studio-apartment. The studio is the living room. I have always seen it spotless, like his palette and his work clothes. He has a pure conception of art. Painting is a noble pursuit; dirt, disorder, confusion only make the creation more difficult.

At sixty-two, Borès does not yet have the wide recognition that he deserves and that many painters much younger than he have achieved. As far as fame is concerned he is young. Although appreciated by collectors and museums, his work has not received its full public due. There are several reasons for this slow discovery. First of all is the secretive and proud nature of the artist himself. He is not dramatic in his speech or gestures; his answers are quiet and brief. He seldom laughs but often smiles. In his art he willfully avoids the melodramatic. The second reason is that his art, always representational, has seemed to be against the non-objective current of the time.

He said, "I try to reconcile my need for plastic creation with the sensations felt in contact with reality, and that my visual memory brings to me sooner or later. This is my principal goal, at least the one that *consciously* I try to reach."

In his own art, Borès has preserved a characteristic curious of many Spanish artists—a sense of humor, the gentler expression of the sense of caricature, that uncanny gift of the great artists to see and portray through the exaggeration of individual peculiarities what may be the true essence of things. Goya, Picasso, Miró are the dramatic examples of this sometimes cruel ability to laugh. It is as if the artist's sense of the tragic had to be hastily, brutally stopped by the cauterization of ridicule and wit.

From his early cubist admiration Borès retains a sense of graphic design, but his understructure of form and line is now coated with light and color. Here the seeming calm of his character helps his work. For color needs time to be used completely. Living for his art, Borès gives to his art the time it needs to ripen. He finds in Paris the calm that in passages of his paintings reminds one of the use of color by the impressionists. Their life was less disturbed by the modern tempo; they could pause, observe, and then put onto their canvases those barely perceptible changes of color that are the nostalgic trace of the irreversible passage of time.

NOTES ON THE ILLUSTRATION

Francisco Borès. 1898–. Born, Spain.
Photograph taken in 1955.

112 Borès at work in his fifth-floor walk-up studio in Paris. This painting is from his series of bathers and beaches.

UTRILLO 105

SEGONZAC

111

LAURENCIN

V
FANTASY AND SURREALISM
CHAGALL   ERNST   MASSON   DALI   MIRÓ

CHAGALL

Vence, a tiny walled hilltop village in the south of France, became in the postwar years a center of intense artistic life, attracting artists, dealers, collectors, students, and snobs. Matisse's white and blue chapel is the temple of this new Athens. Vence seems the undisputed capital of that small stretch of Mediterranean coast between Cannes and Nice. Like a rival city-state of the Italian Renaissance, only Vallauris, where Picasso once lived, disputed its dominance.

To visit the Midi has become a fashionable requisite for anyone interested in today's art. The names of Picasso, Braque, Chagall, Léger, and Matisse are heard from the lips of countless tourists disporting themselves on the promenades and beaches. The evocation of these prestigious names confers a stamp of cultural approval upon the lazy, carefree holiday life of the Riviera. A tourist may feel that he has participated in a creative adventure merely by swimming next to Picasso or Chagall. In the Midi these artists have become the nobles of the land. Their wishes are respected, their activities reported; they are a new royalty.

Marc Chagall, an *émigré* from Russia, who has lived in Germany and America, as well as in France, is a relative newcomer; he bought his white villa at Vence in 1949. Marcel Proust once stayed in it, and the studio, a garagelike building next to the house proper, was one used by Paul Valéry, the great poet, when he painted. The two buildings are on the side of a steep hill, and the magnificent well-kept garden is like a gigantic green staircase descending to the entrance gate.

On a large stone terrace in front of the house a garden table was set for tea. I sat with his wife and waited for Chagall to come from his studio. Intense sunlight streaked through the bitter-clean-smelling leaves of the eucalyptus trees. We were surrounded by flowers; the spottiness of their colors combined with the broken-up patterns of light and shadow created a sensation of visually enclosed space.

Valentine, or "Vava," Chagall's second wife, sat at the table ready to pour the tea. She is Russian; her jet-black hair, her black eyes, black blouse, and black slacks accentuated her Oriental beauty. Her regular, rounded features and subdued, flowing gestures expressed a tender, shy gentleness. There was a weary worldliness in her speech, an understanding feminine intelligence supplementing her alert sense of humor. In her Chagall has found the tact and wisdom that he needs to organize and protect his creative life.

His first wife, Bella, was the companion, the inspiration, and the tender protector of his life. Through her and with her he became Chagall, the great artist. They were married from 1915 until her death in New York in 1944. They had one child, a daughter, Ida, a painter who is a passionate admirer of her father.

The short, stocky man who descended the long flight of steps that joined the studio with the terrace was Chagall. He was dressed all in blue; a thin crisscross of red checkered his blue shirt; a rough belt held his baggy blue linen trousers.

Chagall's face was tanned and weatherbeaten, his strong, marked features surrounded by thinning unruly locks of gray hair. His well-muscled, compact body gave a sense of youthful, dynamic vitality, of earthy male vigor. The intimate welding of the extremes, the physical roughness with the spiritual, contributed stature and dimension to his presence.

He smiled when he saw us, a quick, self-conscious smile, his head slightly tilted to one side, like a bird examining a new object from all angles. The sadness of his eyes added, by contrast, intensity to his smile.

His voice, very soft and husky, had the dim hoarseness of many Russian voices. He seemed to speak with the tips of his lips. In whatever language he uses—French, English, German—a strong indestructible Russian accent colors and modifies the sound of each word. He sat down with a sigh. Vava poured the tea. Often during our conversation I noticed the sighs that seemed momentarily to ease some inner pain.

He laughed often; he laughed as though he enjoyed laughter. He seemed to find in it, as in the sigh, a physical release. He has an acute sense of humor, a curious ability to extract fun out of the incongruities of life, like a protective device quickly interposed in order to avoid the underlying sadness. Perhaps, like Figaro, he makes "haste to laugh . . . for fear of being obliged to weep."

As I watched, the rich texture, the variety, the complexity of this man's nature became apparent. He is intensely alert, curious about people and places. Curiosity, the desire to find out, is a sign of interest in life, and interest in life is a sign of youth. He punctuated and interrupted the conversation with direct, down-to-earth questions. Having asked, he awaited the reply with a preformed expression, as though in advance he knew the answer.

The most mobile, revealing lines on his face are the wrinkles on his brow. A high forehead is plowed by five or six sinuous furrows that undulate simultaneously. His emotions may be measured by the intensity and the direction of these exterior ripples. Surprise, interest, suffering, joy, all have their stylized counterparts in the movements of his brow.

With his ability to ask, he has the parallel gift of listening. Few people listen; an artist must. As Chagall listened, his face took on a sad, meditative expression or suddenly, as if kindled by a spark, his eyes lit up, his mouth opened slightly, as though to facilitate the penetration of meaning. His eyelids opened wide, his eyebrows pushed up, as if to clear the path of sight. At those moments his face was the face of a believing child to whom some miraculous fairy tale was being told. This ability to believe the unbelievable, to see the magical, the wonderful, and the unseen, is a gift shared only by the poet, the artist, and the child. Chagall, now seventy-one, has preciously protected and sheltered the spontaneity of his perception. When the child that is within all of us grows up, then we look, think, and are our real age.

"When people tell me how young I look," Chagall said, "I say, 'Yes, yes, I am stupid.' One must be a little bit stupid and then a little bit smart to retain his original purity."

After tea we went ino his sudio, a long white room. In front of his own handiwork, a new Chagall appeared, a much graver, sterner man. A craftsman surrounded with the tools of his trade, he went about his work in a more matter-of-fact way.

Most artists are quiet in the act of creation. They become absorbed; they withdraw from their environment. Chagall sat down at a large drawing table by the single large, low window. From the incredible clutter of pencils, pens, brushes, paints, he selected a brush and meditatively started to draw. Drawing is the most direct expression of a painter's thought. The black line that slowly unwound on the white sheet of paper was a sinuous arabesque, an undulating expression of a sensuous and supple mind. The curve, the curl, the wound-up spring are images of pent-up vitality, of potential growth.

Slowly under my eyes the curve became a woman's body, the outline of the image that is always first in Chagall's mind. As in music, the line that he had drawn was his main theme. Around it he could play melodic variations. His face suddenly close to the paper, he added tiny dots, black galaxies on the milk-white paper. He would squint, draw back his head, add a minute mark, squint again, and with a subtle, barely perceptible flourish contribute a final dot—half smiling, as though amused by his own subtlety.

Of some painted tiles in the studio he said, "What noble materials for the artist to create with: earth and fire. To be worthy of them one must be pure, simple." There is a yearning in Chagall for deeper values, away from the pleasing. He finds that taste is playing a much too important role in art. "Too often art equals taste. Cheese has taste," he added. He spoke of painters whose refined and subdued color harmonies are in good taste, adding contemptuously, "A woman dressed in the colors of their paintings would look smart."

Above all, he admires the great colorists. Monet: "I adore him, he is the greatest." Bonnard: "Now here was a great painter, and *du sérieux*." He passed short judgments on his contemporaries. Braque: "Great painter, very French." Mondrian: "Good taste, charming." Klee: "I adore him." Modigliani, Soutine: "Great painters." Matisse: "He doesn't give a damn for anything or anybody. He is so sure of himself." Giacometti: "He feels the profound forces of nature. He counts."

Two large canvases stood on easels along the greater length of the main studio. The paintings loomed even larger under the low ceiling; enormous, fantastic scenes swirled kaleidoscopically in oceans of solid color, yellow and blue; floating, dancing figures ignored the laws of gravity.

The bouquets of flowers in his paintings resemble gay fireworks in the star-studded sky; the little upside-down huts reel away from our vision as we are projected into space away from the earth. Man and animal inhabit this eerie landscape. But man looks like man only when he loves. Chagall's lovers lie in tender embrace, wrapped in a deep ultramarine shadow, while a fish with a man's hand screechingly fiddles. The violin, the instrument that most easily touches our emotions and nerves, is usually present; this is a man-made sound, pathetic against the "music of the spheres."

Chagall, practically alone among artists, has painted love. He said, "Love is all; it is the beginning." He has tried to represent love as the original creative impulse, and the great consolation of existence. He translates into visual terms the yearning of lovers.

Artists have generally been satisfied in presenting woman as the object of man's desire in a realistic analysis of her naked form. The nude in painting is treated no differently from any other existing thing and, like a tree or an apple, is studied and transformed by aesthetic laws of form, color, composition. Chagall's figures of women are symbols of purity and love, unadorned by the trickeries of costumed sex appeal. His conception of woman has nothing of the naughtiness of such eighteenth-century French painters as Boucher or Fragonard, nor of the perverse sentimentality of Greuze, nor of the matter-of-fact realism of Courbet and Manet, nor of Renoir's glorification of flesh in texture and form, nor of the linear distortion of Matisse and Modigliani.

His concept of life, art, and love is sentimental. He appeals directly to emotion, by-passing reason, but by his humility, conscientiousness, and knowledge of his craft, Chagall bestows pictorial nobility to the banal. The vision of the artist has always raised and transformed the commonplace. The chair of Van Gogh, the apples of Cézanne, the teapot of Braque are the familiars of our everyday reality. Chagall, in re-emphasizing the existence of love, tenderness, sorrow, and joy, denies the trend away from the spiritual in modern art.

The lovers in Chagall paintings, closely, magnetically, protectively tied to each other, create a new entity and live oblivious to the surrounding hostile tumult of the outside world. This privacy demands its own landscape, and in his paintings bouquets are the couches and bowers for his lovers.

"Love is the strongest possible illumination," Chagall said.

"Love is poetry, too. . . . We are love, we are made of love. How can we live otherwise? That is why I now speak of color-love and no longer color-light. Color-love without theories—it does not deceive."

In his simple, direct way he knows wherein lies his delight and through himself knows what pleases humanity in general. The arabesques of his drawing, the gay colors, the flowers, the angels, the funny animals, the fiddlers, the sky, the stars, and the moon are the elements with which he seeks to touch us. They evoke attractive, gay, poetic, happy associations. We are disarmed, and we open to the inner power of his art. In front of a Chagall painting we can participate, we can experience.

In his youth Chagall retouched photographs; his figures, floating through space, illogically juxtaposed, may stem from the double influence of photomontage and poetic fantasy. Perhaps more clearly revealed are the lasting influences of the time he spent as an assistant to a sign-painter. Signs are paintings on a mural scale. Signs are also signals. Their purpose is to arrest, stop, interest, direct, and inform. The visual representation of an object always gives a quicker image than the word. A boot hanging outside a shop affords quicker communication than the word "Bootmaker." We grasp the meaning of a Chagall painting faster that we would a poem. For a man represented upside down is immediately recognizable, but we have difficulty understanding ɯɐu.

Whatever image he uses, Chagall coats it with the splendor of color. His paintings have the lavish richness of icons, the Oriental gift of illumination; nothing is too precious to adorn the object of devotion. As one watches him paint, one realizes that his technique is a slow process of enrichment. The thin layers of paint rubbed, scratched, smoothed onto the canvas with brush, rag, hand, or knife interplay and create an iridescence that only a sensual delight in the act of painting can achieve. For Chagall, *matière* is important. His symbols if carelessly painted would lose their reality, they would stand for generalities; the mark of the artist would be absent.

Chagall said, "Color is all. When color is right, form is right. Color is everything, color is vibration like music; everything is vibration."

His palette of pale yellow wood is one of the richest, gayest, juiciest palettes of any painter. All the colors, the rarest hues, are squeezed out in lavish mounds; one feels the pleasure of squeezing paint.

Like a human being, a Chagall painting reveals its rich complexity only if one has lived with it and in it, in somewhat the way the artist has during its creation. One must look at his paintings closely to experience their full power. After the impact of the over-all effect, there is the joy of the close-up discovery. In this intimate scrutiny, the slightest variation takes on immense importance. We cannot concentrate for a long time; our senses tire quickly and we need, after moments of intense stimulation, periods of rest. Chagall understands this visual secret better than most painters; he draws our interest into a corner where minute details hold it, and when we tire of that, we rest, floating on a calm space of color, until the eye lands on a new small island of quivering life.

This ability to concentrate on a small area is particular to Chagall. The minute scratching of the needle on the copper when he etches, the deposits of ink from the thinnest nib when he draws, the slight variations of brushstrokes when he paints, are all one pattern. In anything that Chagall creates, the smallest touch, mark, stroke, scratch have meaning.

We left the studio to go back to the house. It is like a Chagall museum. In every room, on every wall, hang rare early Chagalls, miraculously saved from Russia, direct contacts with his youth and the sources of his art. If memory fades, if intensity weakens, he has only to look at his early canvases to be recharged with his own emotional energy.

The most cosmopolitan of all painters, Chagall left Russia in 1910 for France, later went to Germany, back to Russia, back to Germany, back to France, from France to America, and back to France. He is the expatriate who has had to carry his inspiration with him.

Throughout his life Chagall's art has changed little. His subject matter has remained, with very slight variations, the same; his manner of applying paint, of drawing, of etching, his way of expressing himself have been strikingly consistent. There seems to be only one way for him to paint.

"Color is in the blood. I think of the blood as the chemical package that nature through your parents has given you. I do not see blood as purely physical.

"Color is a problem that is practically fated, inescapable, it is unsolvable. It has more to do with the birth of a person, with the atmosphere around him, than with culture and environment.

"An artist has a born-color that is in him, in the chemistry of his blood. In certain cases, at certain times, sociological environment, if it resembles the atmospheric environment, may influence a man's born-color, give it a certain illumination. Some of the dramas, the tragedies, the joys in one's home add their little hue to one's born-color. And so on throughout life, changes of residence, of age light up differently the born-color, the way a stage set is lit. But the fundamental does not change."

Later Chagall said to me, "Poetry is your life, the state of your soul. We won't speak of those who have no poetry in them. God gives you poetry, your parents give it to you, but it is not something final. It must be developed. Poetry at first is like a diamond that you have in your pocket, that you found covered with dirt somewhere. You must make it shine. It is dirty and has to be washed, as every child when he is born. This diamond, this poetry that I speak of can be chemical, or plastic, or musical if you were Mozart, or poetic if you were Verlaine or Shakespeare."

The vast spaces of Russia had not been enlightened by culture when Chagall was born in 1889. Vitebsk was a small provincial town where the animal world was never far removed or separated from peasant life.

Even the élite in Russia at that time, the writers, the musicians, the painters who had been exposed to Western civilization, were still a part of a culture not far above the level of the Middle Ages. If Wagner, Cézanne, Proust had lived several centuries earlier, imagine what their art would have been. Something of the contact of Russian art with the primitive forces of nature was felt when Stravinsky's "Sacre du Printemps" rocked civilized Paris.

Chagall has kept the primitive vision of his childhood throughout his life. He was immersed at the crucial, formative age in the intensely naïve and haunting visual world of his Russian-Jewish origin. A sensitive child's mind and imagination were developed and shaped for life by the pictorial drama of religious ritual, the ageless beauty of ceremony, the revelations of the Bible, and the ever-present Russian sense of the fantastic and magical.

Naïve art, folk art, children's art are all expressions of our desire for the supernatural. There is a need in us for make-believe, for illusion. Theater is make-believe; art is make-believe. A sense of the theatrical, of the magic of the theater is one of the principal elements of art. Chagall has designed many theater and ballet sets. His costumes and décor for *Aleko,* for *The Firebird* were his paintings transposed into a three-dimensional world, and his paintings are stages for the play of his imagination.

After my visit to Vence, I met Chagall again at his daughter's house in Paris. He told me that he was still working on his monumental task of illustrating the Bible, which in 1923 Vollard had asked him to do.

One of the major creative efforts of our time, this illustrated Bible, when finally published in 1956, placed Chagall among the greatest etchers. He has etched more than three hundred plates. By a miracle, a conscientious craftsman hid the Bible plates during the German occupation. Chagall, at sixty-nine, finished the work he had started over thirty years ago. For over thirty years he lived constantly with the Bible. He was like a tree, his roots underground in this then unseen, unpublished work; the leaves, the fruit, the branches were the color-drenched canvases that the world knew as Chagall.

These unseen roots of the creative man explain so much in Chagall's art. Until the publication of his Bible it was as though the world saw a play in which the actors spoke but their voices could not be heard. The meaning of Chagall is in the Bible. And again his history proves there is no great art without faith.

Because of his background, Chagall could feel emotionally and physically a part of the Bible. His Moses is not the elderly Italian noble of Michelangelo or the athletic Greek statue by Blake, but a familiar to Chagall, a patriarch of the Jews. It is a curious plan of fate that, after all his wanderings, Chagall should have settled in Vence. For the landscapes that he saw in his mind as a child, through readings of the Bible, are the landscapes of the Mediterranean land where he now lives. Chagall in his essence belongs to the Mediterranean, the sea of our culture, the sea of the Bible. He has been to Israel, he has been to Italy, to Greece, bringing back from each voyage precise drawings, notations that confirm and revivify the visions of his memory.

That day in Paris, when we left Ida's house, we drove through the streets on our way to the engraver's. Chagall kept exclaiming, "Look at the light. Look at the light of Paris; a stone from Connecticut would be beautiful to paint in the light of Paris.

"Countries have their own colors, which are preordained. There are countries where there is an absence of color; others have just a trace of color; in others still, the color is completely photographic. No one knows why. It is an unsolved problem."

The engraver's atelier was a small two-storied building in a narrow street, far from the vibrations of traffic. Inside, the walls were covered with the prized works that had been produced there. Next to etchings by Léger, Segonzac, and Chagall hung second-rate works. It seems as though without second-rate art there would be no great art; the abundance of art in Paris, regardless of quality, is a fertilizer to art in general.

Only in Paris can one still find a few craftsmen with manual ability equal to that of the artist. One of the reasons why Paris has attracted artists is because at some moment in the execution of their works of art they need that skilled manual help. Painters, sculptors, etchers, designers can still find assistance among that élite of the working classes, the master craftsmen.

We went upstairs to a little room where a window opened onto a sunny garden. On a small table, white gauze stretched on a frame screened the distracting view and equalized the light. Chagall took off his vest. In a workman's shirt, he attacked the dull copper plate lying flat on the table. He picked up a proof and pointed out, using musical terms, "There must be the same black accents everywhere; 're-echoes,' that's the word.

"Black and white is a color. If you do not see color in a black and white picture, it is dead. In Rembrandt, Goya, and Daumier you can see the color in black and white, less so in the others. Matisse has a beautiful black and white because he was a colorist."

To be able to see the barely visible scratches, he put on thin-rimmed glasses, quickly hiding them with the vanity of a man refusing to submit to the image of age. Again, as in his studio in Vence, the subtlest nuances acquired meaning. The eye and the mind must learn to concentrate fixedly on minute detail, while con-

stantly retaining the grand over-all conception. This mental gymnastic is par
of the infinite difficulty of art, the system of checks and balances where the tedium
of execution slows down the impetuous flight of creation.

In the presence of his *chef-d'œuvre,* the real Chagall emerged, a great and
profound religious painter, in the tradition of Rembrandt. When Chagall
finished his morning's work, his last fervent plea, his passionate cue to the en
graver, gave the key to his conception: "It must sing, it must cry; it is the Bible."

Chagall's great gift is literally the power of imagination, the ability to sum
mon and exteriorize on canvas, or other mediums, the substance of dreams, the
intangible mirages of the mind. The visions of this one man's night, exposed bu
undissolved by the light of day, are poised as though ready to lodge themselves and
live in the dreams of those who set eyes upon them. And see them we must, fo
the artist knows the human hunger for color, and the intense jarring colors in
a Chagall painting are illuminated signs that arrest our attention. Like a psycholo
gist conducting visual tests, he knows the power of surprise; our senses routinel·
scanning an expected image are suddenly awakened by the unexpected.

He also knows the power of curiosity, the pleasure of investigating for one·
self, and the self-confirming, egotistical urge to correct mistakes. The gree·
woman with blue hair is an apparent, flagrant error in representing reality, bu
it is also a visual trap set for us by the wily artist. For while the mind is busil·
analyzing, transposing, correcting, our interest is held on the canvas, and all the
while we are experiencing, we are involved.

Chagall's paintings obey only the laws of his own emotion. Chagall explained
"The presence of real objects is a nightmare for me. I have always overturned
objects. A chair or table turned upside down gives me peace and satisfaction. A
man or figure overturned gives me pleasure. . . .

"I had the need not to destroy but to shift things. So I cut off heads, for ex
ample, and put them in impossible places. I upset in order to find, at all cost
another reality."

But the structure of Chagall's mind is against all constraint. As opposed to
the logical, he establishes the equal rights of the illogical. The ordinary man'
reason, presented with the illogical, protectively dismisses it as unimportant; only
logic seems a solid base on which to build. Logical reasoning is a step-by-step
process; it is a continuity of thought. On the other hand, the illogical is a
discontinuity, a break, a jump, as though the cogs of thinking have skipped a
notch. That gap, that opening in the solid wall of reason that protects and at the
same time imprisons us, is the hatch of escape into another world.

The flight from the solid, reasonable ground of reality, the belief that there
is something beyond the known, is creative intuition. The poet, the artist make
us leave the ground, and only if we put our faith in them will we experience their
vision. We must sometimes act contrary to reason. The great explorers were poet
who were sustained by their belief in the existence of the unseen. They had faith
and we, in the presence of art that shocks our reason, must have faith. We mus·
have faith in the sincerity of the artist, and in order to experience fully we mus·
let ourselves go, not resist and puncture the images of a poetic world with the
pinpricks of doubt. The miracle of art is to destroy doubt.

Part of the secret power of Chagall's art is in the artist's struggle against al·

he forces that shackle the flight of inspiration and pull man downward. The
oaring, floating, running, jumping images in his paintings are symbols of libera-
ion.

The profound lyricism of Chagall's art is in his dynamic conception; for him
he image of motion is an image of life. And in motion there is the atavistic,
hildish desire to re-experience pleasure. Chagall tends toward a goal which is no
onger the static ideal of form and beauty that for centuries has been the principal
bject of art. His purpose is to express the longing for the ideal in life. Since man
s an idealist, he strives to surpass, to transcend himself. He needs in his striving
ove, faith, religion. In the visionary art of Chagall lies the tangible proof of
ne man's struggle with this longing. The artist taps the deepest memory of
umanity, where there linger, left from the whole long life of mankind, the forgotten and consciously unknown blissful images. When an artist tries to bring to
he surface these memories, one can judge the man and the artist by the grandeur
f his attempt. Without art, without artistic creation man would have no material
race of his idealism. An artist is a man who can express this so that all men in
heir hearts, souls, and minds feel, know, and see that sublime instant of creation
hen "God saw everything that he had/made, and,/behold, it was very good."

NOTES ON THE ILLUSTRATIONS

Marc Chagall. 1889–. Born, Russia.
Photographs taken in 1952, 1954, 1957, 1958.

13 *Madonna with Sleigh,* 1947. Oil, 38¼″ × 31¼″. Collection Mme. Ida Chagall,
Paris.

14 Chagall laughing; at tea in his Vence garden with his wife.

15 Chagall in his Vence studio. The illusion created by the enormous canvases
transformed the studio into an unreal, poetic world, lit by overpowering
color. The figures seemed to leave the canvases momentarily and to float,
soar, and dance around Chagall as he stood enveloped in the visions he had
evoked. On the left, a section of *La Danse,* 1950–1952.

16 *Elijah's Vision.* Plate 88 for the Bible, 1956. Etching. The Museum of Modern
Art, New York.

17 At work on his Bible illustrations, Chagall examines a plate.

18 A severe craftsman checking proofs for his Bible.

19 A. Paris: The Seine, in front of his Quai Bourbon apartment.
B. Paris: On the mantelpiece, among family photographs, a tile with an ara-
besque and a Delacroix drawing.
C. Paris: Chagall standing before one of his great compositions, *Le Grand
Cirque,* 1956, his own head a part of the painting.

D. Vence: The clutter on his studio desk.
E. Paris: With an early portrait of his father—"Papatchka," or "little father," Chagall said.
F. Vence: A studio shelf with ceramics painted by Chagall.
G. Vence: Chagall with one of his stone carvings.
H. Vence: The exterior of his villa, Les Collines.
I. Vence: His palette is one of the richest of any painter's.
J. New York: Designing costumes for *Daphnis and Chloe.*
K. Paris: In front of *Cantique,* 1957, from his late Paris period.
L. Vence: In the bedroom, left, a Russian icon; in the center, a Bonnard drawing; right, an early cubist Chagall gouache.

ERNST

Max Ernst brings to painting a mind trained in philosophy. From the earliest days of dada and surrealism, he has juxtaposed images as intricately as thinkers juxtapose thoughts. His inventiveness opens new visual horizons. His experiments with technical means lead to a hitherto unknown pictorial language of textures.

His studio is in Huismes, about three hundred kilometers from Paris. The Loire countryside is the true image of *douce France.* Flowers surround the studio in a remodeled farmhouse. In this idyllic, tender scene of nature, Ernst's creations seem the materializations of an alchemist's search. His Gothic features, the white, silky long hair, his self-conscious and studied manner all increase the impression of a visual link with the medieval past. The paintings and the still expression of his eyes made me feel that he had studied the cabala.

NOTES ON THE ILLUSTRATIONS

Max Ernst. 1891–. Born, Germany.
Photographs taken in 1959.

120 Max Ernst in his Huismes studio in 1959. Next to the painting on the easel a stand with paper palettes. Ernst pioneered in the textural surface research of modern painting, his inventive mind constantly ready to find and exploit the yet undiscovered.

121 *Snowblossoms.* Oil, $51\frac{1}{8}'' \times 51\frac{1}{8}''$. Collection Fernand Graindorge, Liège.

MASSON

The studio of André Masson in Aix-en-Provence has the bareness, the intimacy of a Provençal farmhouse. The view from this studio is dominated by Cézanne's Mont Sainte-Victoire. "Since Cézanne," Masson said, "one feels too much in painting the obsession with volume and monumentality. Oil painting is too heavy. I want to deliver the world from gravity."

The son of rich peasants, Masson is rugged, yet gentle. There is nothing harsh in his speech or his gestures. Somehow, the peace of country life has slowly stripped him of defenses. He seems to be a quivering receiving center for the translation of visual impulses. I have seldom seen such exposed sensitivity. He uses this state to pursue his research. Masson is constantly trying to find better means and newer mediums. When I saw him last, he was experimenting with throwing sand and fixing the obtained design.

"I want to create a cosmogony, to remove objects from their familiar and useful situations." He pointed to a painting of nudes. "In this painting I wanted to represent the effort of taking off into flight—beings who are rooted, but have wings and want to fly away. I wanted to project the nudes into a space in which they could live freely. Cosmogony! If I could explain it in words, I would write instead of painting. I want to paint the birth of things, to represent the act, the effort of creation. It is more important than the painting. The painting—it is up to the spectator to make it. The artist must work with the thought that the spectator can understand things half said, not completely described. Just because a spectator is slow, the artist does not have to be slow. One must be understood, but not at any cost. I must hope that the spectator will understand the seed I have offered him."

NOTES ON THE ILLUSTRATION

André Masson. 1896–. Born, France.
Photograph taken in 1956.

122 Masson between two easels in his Aix-en-Provence studio. He is working practically at the same time in two different manners. Left, a semi-realistic painting of nudes, and, right, an experiment in throwing paint and sand. Masson was one of the first French artists to investigate the action of chance· through the throwing of paint.

DALI

Salvador Dali's incredible gestures in art and in life are extensions into space of his inner being. To him the incredible is always possible, and he is sure to try to make it happen. This brilliant intelligence is ready at any time to jolt the conventional and the complacent. Art to him is a tool for opening new horizons to man's imagination. He is a sum of contradictions held together by aesthetic passion. Mysticism, anarchism, surrealism, classicism, expressionism are all reduced to one simple result, Daliism. He surrounds himself with an air of mystery. His long hair "à la Velásquez," his gold-tipped cane, his aggressive mustache pointing to his piercing, steely eyes, his purposely difficult to comprehend speech—all contribute to the spectacle of what he believes the image of an artist caught in life should be. His wife, Gala, ever present in his art and in his life, is the approving and inspiring partner in this unique collaboration between husband and wife on the art stage of the world.

Salvador Dali. 1904–. Born, Spain.
Photographs taken in 1959.

123 Salvador Dali with his wife, Gala.

124 *Saint George and the Dragon,* 1947. Etching, 17⅝" × 11¼". The Museum of Modern Art, New York.

MIRÓ

Joan Miró has no studio in Paris. The closest he comes to one is the Mourlot lithographic atelier, where he creates his unique language of signs. His lithographs belong in the hierarchy of Miró's work and are a major achievement. A few years ago he won the Grand Prix at the Venice Biennale for his graphic work. When saw him in 1953, he sat framed in an alcove and surrounded with first proofs of some new lithographs fresh off the presses. Rotund, short, he easily breaks out into a kind, witty, innocent smile, but his gestures are formal and stylized, as if he were in a Guignol show. This stylized approach to spontaneous humor is the essence of Miró the man, the artist. He seems sometimes to be smiling at imaginary puns. The pun is a reviving somersault of humor, and Miró's drawings themselves are visual puns. His smile, as suddenly as it comes, disappears, and he withdraws from the reality around him into a haughty absence. His face and body take on the forbidding stiffness and severity that only the Spanish can achieve, a mixture of arrogance and humility, arrogance toward life, humility toward death. Miró's humor, like a ray from the sun, fights off the ever-encroaching darkness and sadness in his Spanish temperament.

NOTES ON THE ILLUSTRATION

Joan Miró. 1893–. Born, Spain.
Photograph taken in 1953.

125 Miró at work on lithographs in the Paris atelier of the Mourlot brothers. I is in large part due to the Mourlots that the lithograph has grown in impor tance and become a major art. The love that the Mourlots have for their craft they have instilled in their highly trained artisans. To insure the best presentation of their vision, the artists of the world come to this atelier.

CHAGALL 11

CHAGALL 115

117

CHAGALL

118

CHAGALL 119

A   B

C   D

E   F

G H

I J

K L

121

120 ERNST

DALI 123   124

VI
THE NEW GENERATION
GIACOMETTI   HARTUNG   DUBUFFET   RICHIER   BAZAINE   MANESSIER

GIACOMETTI

Alberto Giacometti is a wiry man, about five feet ten. His face is that of a *condottiere;* thick, curly brown hair encases his head like medieval headgear. The long, straight, noble nose, the deep creases from cheek to thick-lipped mouth, engrave his portrait sharply in my memory.

In the movement of his body there is the weight of gravity. He stands with courage and boldness in front of his easel, in front of his sculpture. His legs, like those of a fighter in a ring, are astride and firmly planted. As he works he springs forward, steps back, scratches his hair.

In his painting everything is reduced to the simplest means of expression: the heads are so small, the nudes and figures so narrow, the brushes so thin. With two fingers he holds a long sable brush at its farthest extremity. He digs it into a tiny layer of gray and white paint. Then, with circular, groping movements, as though in a trance, he shapes a small layer of paint into the suggestion of a face in its minuscule form. His eyes are half closed, his movements rapid. He smokes incessantly. Hundreds of cigarette butts litter the floor. When he sculpts, there is more movement and abandon. He seems to dance around the emerging form. His arms sway wide to add by touch the substance that will be form.

Giacometti lives in an artists' community in one of the sadder parts of Paris. Into a narrow courtyard, some six feet wide and forty feet long, open the doors and windows of various studios. Several garbage cans stand just behind the entrance to the court. On the soot-covered gray stucco walls hang classic bas-reliefs of angels dancing in a frieze, leftovers from more academic inhabitants. Giacometti has the four small studios on each side of the entrance. On the left is the room in which he works, and, next to it, his one-room apartment; across the narrow gap are his brother's workshops, where the processing of Giacometti's sculpture is done. He has lived here since 1927.

His studio is a small room, about fifteen feet by twelve. One window takes up a whole wall. Since the studio is on the ground floor and the courtyard is only six feet wide, the light that streams in is gray and dull. The over-all impression is of monochromatic grayness. The street outside, the whole quarter is gray. The walls are gray; the sculpture gray and white, interspersed with the sepia accent of wood or the dull glint of bronze. The walls are scratched and scribbled on as though some cave painter had tried to capture images in this cavern. Under the big window is a long table entirely covered with squeezed tubes of paint, palettes,

126 GIACOMETTI   277

paint-brushes, rags, bottles of turpentine. Like figures, the bottles stand shrouded in layers of dust chipped away from Giacometti's sculpture. Here sculpture and painting mix intimately. He has painted his recent sculpture in the manner of the ancient Greeks, and on his worktable the two mediums intermingle—turpentine, oil paint, color-soaked plaster, with clay, wire, stone, and bronze.

In the darker corners of the room his long, narrow life-size figures of white plaster seem like apparitions from another planet. One is surrounded by beings never encountered before. In other statues he has shriveled the human form to its smallest visible image. Men and women one-quarter of an inch tall stand on monumental pedestals. This ability to suggest dimension is one of Giacometti's chief preoccupations.

Giacometti is obsessed with the unattainable. "One does that which escapes one most," he said. How thin, how without substance can the human body be? How small, how infinitesimal? How to express in art an idea, the idea, the concept of man? An idea is something immaterial; one must use the minimum of material substance, reduce the quantity of substance needed to express an idea to the limit. This fantastic economy of means is at the heart of Giacometti's work: the minimum of color, the minimum of texture, the minimum of substance. It's as though the structure inside his sculpture were the idea of the sculpture itself. And when there is so little, every accident, every grain of matter on his long bodies take on a profound meaning.

"Why does one paint or sculpt?" he said. "It's the need to dominate things, and one can only dominate by understanding. I make a head to understand how I see, not to make a work of art. One must understand through intuition what moves one, and arrive at domination through logic, not through science. Art is not a science." As Giacometti talked, he worked on a clay torso and head. It seemed to take on the shape of the many portraits he has done of his brother Diego, as though his brother's head were an ever-present form in his mind. As usual he worked on doubtfully, complainingly, as if unable to predict the result of his work. He suddenly stopped and said with despair, "It looks like an object— a dead object."

Obsessed with line, he is also obsessed with jotting down and capturing images wherever and whenever he can. In the corners of his studios lie many portfolios of paper on which he draws with charcoal, pencil, oil, ink, any medium. His walls are covered with drawings, his sketchbooks full. He said, "I've been fifty thousand times to the Louvre. I have copied everything in drawing, trying to understand. Art is more what one sees than what one reads."

He spoke of the duality of precision—imprecision. "Look at an Egyptian head. It's precise, but its effect is mysterious. Venus de Milo means nothing to me, but I like Phidias and the archaic Greeks. *Laocoön* fascinates me."

About the creative impulse he said, "No one decides 'I'm going to do sculpture,' or 'I'm going to do painting.' One just does it. It's an absurd activity. One does things through mania, obsession, through an automatic need that escapes the understanding."

On the walls of his bedroom are drawings, and the cracked paint on the cupboards reminds one of damaged frescoes. In this room there is a bed with no back, just a mattress with an eiderdown, two pillows, and white sheets. An ordinary painted chair, the paint all cracked on its rounded, bent back, serves as a bed table. On it were three or four torn books of poems: Apollinaire's *Alcools* and the poetry of Rimbaud. Like Matisse, Braque, and Picasso, Giacometti is a great reader of poetry. But unlike many artists, he reads innumerable newspapers. Behind the bed are an old wireless set, a small lamp, a large, badly painted closet. Next to two jars of instant coffee stand empty jars of yogurt. Diagonally across one corner of the room hangs a string on which clothes and kitchen towels dry. Under the window is a sink, a small two-plate burner, a basin, a pitcher of flowers. The small bouquet that his wife places in their sad, grim bedroom is a spark of emotional relief. Without it this room would seem unbearable.

Giacometti's wife, Annette, is about five feet four, like a slender girl of fourteen. She is not fourteen, she is much older, but her youth, her beauty, a poetic quality of mood are a contrast to Giacometti's somber brooding. She has the naïve and innocent expression of a child, and laughs often with a girl's laughter. This girl-wife seems made to be the companion who does not distract the artist from his work. They met in 1949. She always says the formal *vous* to Giacometti. He sometimes teases her. Then the wrinkles, the two deep furrows in Giacometti's face crease even deeper, and he beams like a mountaineer enjoying a good joke.

He is a man possessed. Time has no meaning in his daily life; he eats and sleeps as he needs to. There is no specific hour for any activity, only the time to speak, to create. He creates best at night. He has been known to work through forty-eight hours without sleep or meals. His best work, he believes, is done after hours and hours of work, when he is so tired that his intelligence has lost control. This is a familiar feeling of many artists, this extraordinary state of trance that can be obtained only through extreme physical fatigue. Then, exhausted, Giacometti lies on his bed and says, "I don't know. What am I going to do? The work is not coming as it should. I will soon have to look for another métier if it goes on like this." To get away from his self-torture, Giacometti often visits his mother in southern Switzerland, near the Italian border. (His father was a famous Swiss post-impressionist painter who had studied with Bouguereau.) There, for several weeks or months, in a small village, he stays immersed in nature, sketching endlessly.

It is strange that this famous man, one of the great sculptors and painters of our day, lives the way he does. This misery is not materially necessary, but perhaps there is a superstitious need to prolong the mood of his creative inspiration. Looking at his small, crowded studio, Giacometti said, "I've never had the time to move. The more I work the bigger this studio seems." To relocate and adjust physically and suddenly to improved quarters might cut the thread, alter the radioactive effect of the surroundings that have produced so many masterpieces. Here Giacometti has found his own world, a world of stone, a world of dust—everything is dust. This dust is the substance out of which God fashioned the universe and out of which Giacometti fashions his own universe. To move a bottle, to clean up the studio, might be sacrilege.

Cézanne toward the end of his life expressed the anguish of the truly creative artist. "I have not realized," he wrote. Giacometti is such an artist. He is obsessed with the pursuit of the ideal. Never satisfied, he smashes or discards much of his work. "I have always failed . . . but I am sure no one can realize that for which he strives! . . . Oh, to be able to say, 'That's it, I cannot do more.' "

NOTES ON THE ILLUSTRATIONS

Alberto Giacometti. 1901–1966. Born, Switzerland.
Photographs taken in 1951, 1953, 1954, 1955.

126 *Diego,* 1954. Oil, $31\frac{7}{8}'' \times 25\frac{9}{16}''$. Galerie Maeght, Paris.

127 Sculptor-painter Alberto Giacometti in his Paris studio, standing in front of his easel, his sculpure behind him.

128 *Figure,* 1951. Pencil. Private collection, New York.

129 Giacometti and his wife, playing with a newborn kitten.

130 A. The alley that separates Giacometti's studio, right, from his casting studio, left, where his brother Diego helps him.
B. The walls of Giacometti's small studio are covered with his drawings. On a shelf are many works in progress.
C. Giacometti working on a bust of his brother Diego.
D. Concentration.
E. Finished and unfinished sculptures, mysterious hieratic forms shrouded in his studio.
F. In his tiny one-room kitchen-bedroom-living room, on a chair by the bed, books of poems by Rimbaud, Apollinaire.
G. Giacometti sculpts standing; he moves around his sculpture.
H. Annette reading in the studio, surrounded by works in progress.
I. In the bedroom, flowers, and drawings on the walls.
J. While he works, a cigarette is never out of his hand.
K. When he paints he holds his thin brushes at the very tip, so that his smallest movement is amplified.
L. The artist's family, his wife Annette, brother Diego.

131 In the stillness of Giacometti's studio. Bottles of turpentine stand beside his small figures; outside, a frieze of classic angels.

HARTUNG

Hans Hartung is a painter of line, as others are painters of color. In Oriental calligraphy a cultivated mind could express itself; in the automatism of Hartung's obsessive sign-making the personality of the artist is absorbed in the anonymity of a moment in time.

The white sheet of paper framed in black was ready like a screen for the projection of Hartung's vision. There were minutes of intense quiet suddenly shattered by the piercing, hissing sound of his crayon on stretched paper. The violence and speed of his work made it seem like an outpouring of pent-up urge. Then the drawing was finished, the briefness of execution adding mystery to the intensity of the experience.

NOTES ON THE ILLUSTRATIONS

Hans Hartung, 1904—. Born, Germany.
Photographs taken in 1959.

132 Hartung works sitting down. He lost a leg in World War II.

133 *No. 77, 1959*. Lithograph. Museum of Modern Art.

DUBUFFET

The origin of pictorial vocations is mysterious and varied. Jean Dubuffet was a wine dealer, then a maker of theatrical masks. He assaults the concept of beauty with the violence of a primitive. A compulsive belief that truth can be found in untrained vision makes him investigate the arts of the innocent—children, savages, madmen, and the unconscious everyday artists who scribble on walls. These outpourings of instinct, however distorted, are the undecoded messages from man's inner yearnings.

It is hard to penetrate Dubuffet's shell of self-protection from everyday life; he knowingly shelters his inner dreams. He looks like a being who could have lived untold years ago. With something of a medium's power Dubuffet links in his art the far-distant past with the unseen—to all but him—future. He has broken more violently with the conventions of traditional easel painting than any painter I have photographed. I watched him throw sand, or gravel, into amorphous mixtures smeared over a plaster board. With a knife, trowel, rag, or his hand, he shaped the lavalike flows of earth color until he finally brought them to a stop. I marveled at the amount of stored-up skill he summoned to fix the fleeting images that seemed to well up like volcanic eruptions.

NOTES ON THE ILLUSTRATIONS

Jean Dubuffet. 1901—. Born, France.
Photographs taken in 1952.

134 *Head with Lilac Nose,* 1951. Oil, 32″ × 25½″. Collection Mr. and Mrs. Ralph Colin, New York.

135 Portrait of Jean Dubuffet. He likes to wear blue jeans when working.

136 The painter in action. Dubuffet makes movement and speed participate in the creation of his paintings. He has abandoned traditional tools.

RICHIER

This great woman sculptor clung to the human image, as if intuitively she sensed that birth and man are results of earth's fertility, nature's creativity. Her use of organic forms, leaves, branches emphasizes this profound harmony. In a space age she stressed the metamorphosis of earth-bound living matter into the spiritual.

These are the last photographs taken of Germaine Richier. She seemed so happy, so full of life and plans. A woman of the South, she spoke French with the ripe accent of the Midi. She punctuated her meaning with the exuberant mimicry and generosity of gesture true to the Méridional. Her studio was clean and luminous; her tools were neatly and precisely arranged. She wore a spotless blue jacket and on it the bright red accent of the Legion of Honor. Kindness radiated around her. She made me want to stay. In her presence one believed in the superior power of love.

NOTES ON THE ILLUSTRATIONS

Germaine Richier. 1904–1959. Born, France.
Photographs taken in 1959.

137 The tools of Richier's studio, instruments of support, control, order, and measure. They hang next to a vast accumulation of unorganized matter, dried-up tree branches, herbs, shells, skeletons of bats and frogs, bones, the inorganic substance of inspiration from which the great sculptor created. On the right, a sculpture, *L'Homme-forêt,* 1945.

138 Germaine Richier in her studio next to her sculpture, *The Ogre.*

BAZAINE

Jean Bazaine came from Lorraine ancestry. In his youth he studied literature and sculpture before discovering painting. His young, lean face contrasts with his prematurely white hair. The whole image is of tense, adventurous wisdom.

He built himself a studio on the outskirts of Paris—the old Zone where the *clochards* managed to exist in makeshift misery. He said, "I paint because I can't help painting; otherwise I would take care of children or have a farm in the country."

One of the most intellectual painters of the new generation, he is deeply immersed in the problems that have interested all serious artists. The belief in the existence of great laws hidden beneath the diversity of everyday appearance is the core of Bazaine's art. With the fanaticism of a scientist searching to solve a riddle of life, he studies, draws, restudies, redraws hundreds of times the simplest forms about us—rocks, leaves. Somewhere there must be a unity; the artist as the foreseer for humanity may be the one to reveal it.

Bazaine is a painter who uses the effect that only paint can give. Near his easel are hundreds of discarded razor blades with which he scratches and re-scratches each layer of paint until only the thinnest covering remains. Each film changes the underlying form, much as the changes of climate leave their mark on nature. The painter telescopes centuries of deposits and erosion in the quick process of his work. The finished painting is the record of the personal climate of the artist.

"I do not know what direction modern art will take! But when I see the direction the world is taking I am worried for painting."

NOTES ON THE ILLUSTRATIONS

Jean Bazaine. 1904–. Born, France.
Photographs taken in 1956, 1958.

139 On a wall of Bazaine's Paris studio, reproductions of art masterpieces of his choice mixed with family portraits of his parents and his daughter. There are several Cézannes—bathers, still lifes, and portraits—and, unexpectedly, a detail from Van Eyck's Arnolfini portrait. On the upper right, a photograph of Father Couturier, who was the great link between modern art and the Church in France. Under his inspiration, Bazaine made mosaics and stained-glass windows for churches.

140 Jean Bazaine at ease in his studio garden on the outskirts of Paris. At work he wears old, sometimes torn clothes.

141 Interior of Bazaine's studio. On the wall, several preparatory pen-and-ink, pencil, and water-color studies. On the easels, paintings he was working on. Bazaine progressively abstracts reality. Only the memory guide lines remain in the finished work.

MANESSIER

Alfred Manessier at forty-nine seems much younger than his age. At first he looks like a man who lives out of doors, for his body is lean and athletic, typical of his French generation that is increasingly conscious of sports. He is calm and speaks clearly and simply. His northern French ancestry deceptively gives him a serene exterior, covering with slowness of gesture and facial immobility his temperament.

The years of war changed the cultural life of Paris. Links with tradition were severed, and in the troubled postwar period old values were reappraised. In the surrounding agitation Manessier discovered permanent, profound values. In 1942 he underwent a deep religious experience after a retreat in a Trappist monastery. Since then he has found in active Catholic faith his real subject matter, the inexpressible aspirations of the soul. In his vast top-floor studio he pursues his "meditation in paint." Manessier's mysticism is as real to him as nature is to other painters. If his painting seems to have no recognizable link with the world that surrounds us, this is because it stems from the secret imagery of his inner reality. Other painters abstract from nature, he abstracts from imagination. His religious preoccupation dominates his life and his art.

Manessier said, "To my mind, modern art is dividing itself in three directions. One, essentially optimistic, accepts without reservation the great modern scientific current and attempts to arrange the world materially and to insure comfort and happiness in an implacable order; it is by necessity insensitive.

"The second direction is the opposite and stems from total rejection and complete individual pessimism. It emits its tragic cry haphazardly to the point of sneering absurdity, all nerves exposed and all colors ejected and streaming.

"The third direction, it seems to me, is the one for Christians; for those who proclaim the importance of heart and love in this world in which these two things are so awkward and embarrassing. . . . It is 'Tragic Optimism.' " This third way is the direction of Manessier's art.

NOTES ON THE ILLUSTRATION

Alfred Manessier. 1911–. Born, France.
Photograph taken in 1958.

142 The artist and his family. He is shown with his wife, his children, and his mother. Behind them, Manessier's *Paysage Aérien,* 1953. The whole scene is dominated by the ever-present symbol of his faith, the cross.

Manessier is a meticulous craftsman who mixes his own paint. In bottles on the window sill of his studio he keeps oil exposed to the sun to bleach it. Under another wooden cross are reproductions of works he admires, a Rembrandt, a Corot—the god of many modern French artists.

GIACOMETTI

GIACOMETTI 130

A   B

C   D

E   F

G H

I J
K L

134

DUBUFFET

135

RICHIER 137

BAZAINE 141